GOD'S BRAINWAVE

GOD'S BRAINWAVE

the story of Jesus doing the job his
old Dad sent him to do

by

BERNARD MILES

HODDER AND STOUGHTON

Printed in Great Britain
for Hodder and Stoughton Limited,
St. Paul's House, Warwick Lane, London, E.C.4,
by Richard Clay (The Chaucer Press), Ltd.,
Bungay, Suffolk

To my sisters
Enid and Kathleen
with love and gratitude

PREFACE

Six years ago, when I joined the BBC's Religious Broad-casting Department, I began to wonder how the New Testament might be broadcast in a form that would be contemporary, startling, compulsive and offensive only in the sense that when the words of Jesus really come home, they *are* so often offensive.

I worried at this for more than two years, asking various people to try their hand at a sample script. I was getting nowhere: some were too near the Authorised Version, others too 'way out', and I began to feel I would never find the right person for the job. Then, one evening, I asked my secretary to get out of the library all the records of Bernard Miles telling his Hertfordshire stories—I vaguely remembered that some of them were about local church characters. I listened the whole of that evening to Bernard Miles on disc. He made me laugh, he held my attention and, as I had suspected, there were many stories that contained sharp words of homely wisdom set in the context of local church life.

I knew that he was my man so I went to see him. He listened patiently as I outlined my scheme of thirty five-minute broadcasts telling the story of Jesus. He was very polite but gave me an adamant 'no'. He couldn't call himself an out-and-out Christian; the best he could say was that he was working his way up the ladder and making steady progress! And in any event he shrank from the role of preacher. No, he wasn't interested. But as I was leaving, his wife told me not to give up as she felt that in his heart he would really love to do it. So I called on him again several times, always on the same errand, always getting the same answer, until one day he said, 'But Roy, think of the work involved. I don't know how I could ever find the time.' I knew then that he was considering the project as a real possibility and left it at that.

Fifteen months after I first went to see him there arrived on my desk a large envelope containing the first draft of thirty scripts written by Bernard Miles and Harry Ibbetson in collaboration. I took them home that night and read them at one sitting. They were exactly what I had hoped for. Here was the story of Jesus; here in a startling version was an accurate paraphrase of the Gospels.

But here and there, written into the scripts, were the occasional swear-words. Bernard argued, and I agreed, that if the character of Jesus was to be seen as authentic, then the people around him must also be authentic. Water down the portrayal of the people around him and you would be watering down Jesus himself. But we were careful to ensure that words which might shock some listeners were only included if, without them, the story would be made to sound artificial or unreal. What would a rough Roman soldier have said when he struck Jesus in the face? How would Jesus really have spoken when he lost his temper with the riff-raff in the Temple?

The day came to start the recordings. After many hours of hard work on the scripts the moment had come to get them down on tape. Bernard was in position in the studio and we were all set to go when he signalled to me over the inter-com between studio and control room and said, 'Now, down on your knees, lads. This is the moment of truth!' He then spoke very simply Sir Thomas Astley's prayer before the battle of Naseby: 'Oh Lord, we have work to do today. If we forget Thee, do not Thou forget us.'

That our prayer was answered I believe this book to be a witness.

Roy Trevivian

ACKNOWLEDGEMENT

WHEN I realised I should never find time to do the whole job myself I got my old friend, Essex-born Harry Ibbetson, to make a set of drafts which I then began to work over, fitting them to my own Hertfordshire tongue, so similar to his East Anglian, yet so very different, and adding dozens of phrases learned from my Buckinghamshire father and Scottish mother fifty years ago.

The present version is identical with the broadcast version except for the elimination of actual dialogue spellings, and phrases linking one broadcast episode with the next.

To Harry Ibbetson, therefore, and to BBC's Roy Trevivian, who guided me so sympathetically through the recording sessions, to his beautiful secretary, Pat, who typed three or four complete versions of the text, and to Garry Clark and Peter Watts who made Decca's Ace of Clubs recording of some of the book, my warm and grateful thanks.

BERNARD MILES

CONTENTS

FOREWORD

I DREAMT I was walking with Jesus by the shores of Galilee and we were talking together like old mates.

'You did a good job with those Gospel talks,' he said. 'And I'm right proud of you. But I hear you had a spot of trouble with the lads at the broadcasting place.'

'Not what you'd call bother, Master, only a little argument over a matter of principle. As you know, the story, as I conceived it, is told by a simple working fellow not unlike one of your twelve mates and I wanted to put in one or two swear-words to make it a bit more realistic and bring it home to people. I argued that when you got your rag out in the Temple you must have spoken pretty forcibly.'

'I did, indeed,' said Jesus, smiling at the recollection. 'I really let them have it.'

'And when you were up in front of the high priests, and those fellows had hold of you, I argued that they must have used pretty foul language.'

'I never heard language like it.'

'So I put a few so-called "swear-words" into the mouths of several of the characters. Even into yours. Words like a miner would use, or a steel worker, or a chap on a farm.'

I whispered one or two of the actual words.

'Those are just the words we did use,' said Jesus.

'You're right on the ball. But you must try to understand the BBC's position; they do their best. They can't afford to be too Christian or they'd be way out in the ratings; they have to steer a middle course. You mustn't expect too much. I agree the words you want to put in are very good and very true, in fact I'd call them bang on. I wasn't very gentle, you know. I couldn't afford to be. It was tough going every step of the way and those blessed pharisees were a pain in the neck.'

'Thanks, Lord,' said I.

And then I woke up, *and of course that's not what Jesus said at all!* But it does show you what I'm trying to get at, bringing it all down to earth and making it real for a lot of people who've never even given it a thought.

B. M.

GOD'S BRAINWAVE

IT was God's idea. When he saw the mess people had got themselves into, all the mistakes they were making and all the trouble they were piling up for themselves, with no-one to help them and show them the proper way to carry on, he reckoned it was about time he took a hand and did something about it.

But he didn't want to send a flood to drown them like he'd done before: and he didn't want to give them another dose of fire and brimstone like he'd done at Sodom and Gomorrah. Because even that hadn't kept them from getting into just the same sort of mess all over again.

But years before, when he'd spoken to Abraham and Isaac and old King David, he'd promised to send them a great leader, someone to look after them and guide them and be their King. And now he decided to keep his promise. Question was who could he trust to do the job aright? It wasn't an easy job you know. It was going to take a bit of doing. But then he had this brainwave. He'd send his own son, give him all his own power and rights, and if that didn't do the trick, nothing would. Might as well shut up shop.

But first of all, he sends one of his head messengers, an old angel called Gabriel, to fix things up and start getting things ready and tell people what to expect.

So old Gabriel comes flying down from Heaven and lands slap, bang, right in front of an old parson called Zachary. Pretty near frightened the poor old fellow out his wits.

But he says, 'Don't be frightened, Zack. I've come down to tell you that your old missus is going to have a baby.'

'Get away,' says old Zachary. 'She's too old for that sort of thing. So am I for that matter.'

'You listen to what I'm saying,' says the angel, 'and don't argue the point. Your old Lizzy is going to have a son.'

'It ain't possible,' says Zachary, 'she's rising sixty, and I'm a damn sight older.'

'That's as may be,' says the old angel. 'But a baby boy she'll have and you're to call him John. And he'll be a preacher, and a teetotaller, and he's going to tell the people about God's son who's soon going to be born. And since you don't seem to believe a word I'm saying you'll be struck dumb till the baby's born. So there!' And off the old angel flies. A bit irritated you see. And sure enough poor old Zachary was struck dumb—he couldn't speak a word to anybody.

Not long after he dropped in to see old Zachary, the old angel pays another call. This time it was to Zack's wife's cousin, young Mary. Now Mary was only a slip of a girl, shy as a mouse and innocent as a lamb. She was walking out with a fellow named Joseph. Going with him regular.

Well, when she saw the angel Gabriel standing there before her, with his wings spread, like a great big kingfisher, all the colours of the rainbow, she was just about as scared as old Zachary had been. And when she heard the angel say, 'Hello, my darling! I got a bit of good news for you!' she didn't exactly know what to make of it. Especially when the old angel goes on to tell her she's going to have a baby. It doesn't seem right to be spoken to like that, even by an angel.

But old Gabriel calms her down, he says, 'And your baby is going to be God's own son, and King of the Jews.' But Mary can't make head or tail of it, for she isn't married. She's never been with a man in her life, not in that way. And she tells him so.

But old Gabriel says, 'Don't you worry your pretty head about that. God'll look after that. There's nothing he can't do. Take your old cousin Lizzie, now. Who'd have thought she'd be carrying at her age? But she's six months gone. God can do anything. You just leave it to him.'

So Mary says, 'If it's God's will, God's will be done. I certainly wouldn't want to stand in his way.'

Now, soon after that she paid a visit to old Lizzie, just to check up and compare notes like. And as soon as old Lizzie heard her come in the front door the baby inside her gave a little jump. She ups and says to Mary, 'Why, Mary, I do believe you're carrying too! As soon as you came in the front door the babe in my belly gave a great big kick, the little devil, bless his little heart! And bless you too, Mary, and may your baby be a blessing to us all!'

And Mary said, ' 'Tis a wonderful thing that's happened to both of us, Lizzie, and I thank God for it with all my heart and soul.'

Well, soon after Mary had left to go home old Lizzie gave birth to a baby boy, and they christened him John like they'd been told. And suddenly old Zachary could speak again, just like the angel had said.

A BABY BOY

But that was nothing to what happened a week or two afterwards, because the time soon came round when Mary was to have her baby. It appears she hadn't told anybody about the old angel coming to see her, so now, when all her clothes start getting a bit tight, she's got some explaining to do.

The fellow she was hitched up to was called Joseph, a carpenter he was, a good steady chap. And they were thinking of getting married—well, it was all fixed up, they'd named the day and everybody was looking forward to it. So of course when he sees she's been got in the family way he takes it wonderful hard. He's never done wrong with her. He wouldn't have thought of such a thing. He's got more respect.

Anyhow, when he sees the way she is he wants to know the why and the wherefore of it, same as you and me would have done. Talks of breaking it off and asking for the ring back. But then one night he has a dream, and in this dream an angel tells him not to worry about Mary, she's a good girl, and she's done no wrong. And the angel goes on to tell him that the child she's carrying is going to be Jesus Christ, the King of the Jews, that they'd all been looking forward to for ages and ages, and that Abraham and Isaac and all the other old prophets had written about donkey's years ago.

Well of course that puts a different complexion on it. When he wakes up out of his dream, he's right proud to think his fiancée's going to be the mother of a king. That's a different kettle of fish altogether.

Well now, just about this time the Government orders a count of heads, what they call a census, the same as we have today, every now and again. All the people have to go back to where they've been born and reared, to be counted, and have their names written down. So's the Government'll know how many people they've got.

So off Joseph has to go, all the way to a little tin-pot place called Bethlehem, where he'd been born, and he takes Mary along with him.

But when he gets there they can't find anywhere to sleep, no lodgings. Everywhere was packed out. They couldn't get a bed for love or money. So poor old Joseph, after knocking at door after door and getting fed up with being turned away, takes Mary out into the countryside, and there they bed down in an old barn. Well, when I say barn it was more like an old cowshed.

And there poor Mary starts her labour, lying on a truss of straw. And there her baby was born. And they tore the lining out of old Joseph's overcoat and wrapped it round the little baby and laid the poor little mite in the cattle manger.

And just across the fields were some shepherds minding their sheep. And suddenly they saw a bright light shining all round them, so bright it dazzled their eyes. They were scared out of their wits, poor old fellows.

Then a voice told them not to be frightened, they weren't going to get hurt. A wonderful thing had happened. Christ the new King had just been born. And if they were to go down and look in the old cowshed they'd see for themselves.

And, as they stood there on the hillside, their poor old wits pretty well addled with the wonder of it, the whole sky suddenly lighted up and burst out singing. They saw a million angels, all singing fit to burst themselves—'Glory be to God, and Peace on Earth!'

Then the light faded out and everything was quiet again. And there the old shepherds stood, pinching themselves to make sure they weren't dreaming. Then one of them said, 'Best go down there and find out what's it all about.'

So down the hill they go, and across the fields to this old cowshed. And when they get there they see a light —old Joseph's lantern, of course. They creep up close, and they look inside, and there they see Mary and her little mite of a child lying in the cattle manger.

And so it came about that two or three rough old working chaps were the first to pay their respects to him. Not kings and queens nor people with a lot of money, and not big men in the church, nor judges nor professors, nor Members of Parliament, but three or four rough old shepherds minding their sheep.

And when they left the cowshed and went off and told people what they'd seen, some believed them and some didn't, just the same as it is today.

But that isn't the end of the story, not by a long chalk. That little baby, lying there in the straw, was to stir up the whole world. Kings would try and murder

him, priests would try and lock him up, his own
countrymen would hunt him down like a wild animal,
and get their teeth into him, and worry him like a dog
worries a rat. More's the pity!

HEROD TRIES TO KNOCK HIM OFF

AFTER Jesus was born, Mary and Joseph got a little cottage and stayed on for a bit. I expect old Joseph got a job as a joiner, or else set up for himself; he's got a family to keep now, you see. Not like the old days when he could do as he liked.

Anyway, as soon as Mary was up and about again he took a day off and they went up to Jerusalem to have little Jesus presented at the Temple, what we'd call 'baptised', only there wasn't such a thing in those days, not till John Baptist started it off.

And in the Temple there was an old old chap named Simeon, a lovely old chap, looking about a hundred and fifty years old, with a long beard and a walking stick and a pair of old spectacles. Oh, he was an age! He takes hold of little Jesus and he says, 'Now I can die in peace. This child is a wonderful sight to my poor old eyes, and I thank God I've lived to see him. This little chap will be the pride and glory of us all! And some will follow him and some won't. But they'd better, else they'll be sorry for it, as sure as eggs are eggs.'

Then he looks into Mary's eyes, and he says, 'And as for you, Missus, I see a load of trouble in store for you. I see heartbreak and sorrow and suffering, all on account of this young lad. But in the end it'll be worth it. You mark my words.'

Then an old girl named Anna came up. She was a sort of fortune teller, could see into the future as well as you and me can see into the back yard. She says much the same thing, that Jesus would be king of the whole world and save all them that followed him.

And they weren't the only ones that knew. There were three wise men, some say they were kings; they knew all about it as well. They lived miles and miles away, right out in the East. They saw a bright star moving across the sky and they followed after it because they'd been told it would lead them straight to where the new King was.

So they followed this star all the way to Jerusalem and there they went into the palace and asked old King Herod where the new King was to be found. But he didn't know. He hadn't heard of any new King. He didn't much like the sound of it when he did hear, either, him being King himself.

Anyway, he makes one or two enquiries and at last someone tells him that the old prophets had said something about a new King being born in Bethlehem. So old Herod tells the three wise men to go there, and if they do find the new King, to be sure and let him know, so that he can come and pay his respects.

So they take the Bethlehem road and off they go. And no sooner had they started when the old star crops up again, leading them straight as a die to where Joseph and Mary and little Jesus were living. It stopped right above the chimney-pot. And when they saw this the three wise men were wonderful pleased, and they clambered down off their camels and in they went.

And inside there was Mary with the little baby lying

in her lap. And down they go on their bended knees, all three of them, thanking God they'd found him at last.

Then they unwrap their parcels and get out the presents they've brought him—a big bag of gold, and a bottle of lavender water, and a jar of nice ointment in case his nappies were chafing him. The first Christmas presents they were, and much the same sort as we give today, only we don't often get bags of gold, worse luck. Well that's against the law, except when its done up into jewellery.

Then, after Mary had given them a bite to eat, they get back on their camels and off they go, back to where they came from. But they don't tell old Herod where Jesus is, they don't say a word to him, because they've got an idea he isn't too keen on the idea of a new little King. He might do the child a mischief.

And they're right, too. Old King Herold only wants to know about Jesus so that he can polish him off quick before he grows up. He's scared little Jesus'll do him out of a job.

But he doesn't get a chance because an angel comes and tips old Joseph off, and him and Mary and Jesus do a moon-light flit, right out of the country, all the way down into Egypt.

And its just as well they do, for what do you think old Herod did? He ordered all the little baby boys for miles around to be knocked off, the wicked old devil. But all to no account, because Joseph's given him the slip, and little Jesus is safe and sound on the other side of the Suez Canal.

THE DEVIL HAS A GO

AFTER Mary and Joseph had been in Egypt a little while, they got word that old Herod had kicked the bucket, so it was safe to come back. But they didn't come back to where he'd been king. No, they went back to Nazareth, and there old Joe set up as a jobbing carpenter.

Now, once every year he takes his family to Jerusalem for their holidays. And one year, when Jesus was about ten or twelve years old, they were just going back, well they were already on the train, when what do you think? Young Jesus was missing. Well, you can imagine what a state poor old Joseph and Mary were in. They searched everywhere, they looked under the seats, they asked the guard, they asked all the passengers. But no, not a sign of him.

So back they went all the way from the station into the town. And there they found him, at the college if you please, sat down among all the scholars and teachers, arguing the point with them, talking his little head off, and them listening to him as if he was the top professor, instead of a little boy of twelve. And of course Mary was so upset she got cross with him. She says, 'What do you mean, upsetting us like this, you naughty boy. We've been looking everywhere for you.'

But Jesus laughed. He says, 'You ought to have known I'd be all right, Mum. You ought to have realised it's time I started doing the job I was sent to do.'

But Joseph and Mary couldn't make head or tail of that. They only knew it was time he was abed. So they bundled him back to Nazareth on the next train.

After that Jesus didn't give them any more trouble. He stayed and helped in the workshop, and he turned out a wonderful good little carpenter. Well, he was doing dove-tail halving joints by the time he was twelve so he must have been pretty good. And he read his books and he grew up to be as fine a lad as you could wish to meet.

Now you remember John, old Zack and Lizzie's son? Well, he was a funny sort of lad. As soon as he grew up he went off to live all by himself like an old gypsy. Lived on what he could pick up from the hedges, nuts and berries and roots and such-like. And folk would come and listen to him preaching, and he'd tell them there was to be a new leader and a great King, and those that wanted to follow this new leader must be sorry for all the mistakes they'd made—what he called repenting —make a fresh start and get themselves born all over again. And then he poured water over their heads, and dipped them in the river, and he called that baptising them, which was like signing them on you see, to follow the new King.

Now by this time Jesus had grown up and he came to where John was busy preaching and baptising, and he wanted John to do him along with all the rest. But old John says, 'You ought to be doing this to me, not the other way round. After all, you're the Guvnor.' But

Jesus wouldn't hear of it. He made John baptise him the same as all the others.

And just as John poured the water over him, there came a flash of lightning and a voice like thunder out of the sky. 'This is my only Son, and a good lad he is. Take notice of what he tells you!'

And a little white dove came flying down and settled on Jesus's head, to show that he had all God's power behind him. And then Jesus left old John and went off by himself to sort things out, what they call meditating. He wandered about the countryside and he went without food for so long he was pretty nearly starving. Weak as a rat he was. And the old Devil saw this and he came wheedling up alongside Jesus and he said, 'If you've got all the power your old man boasted about, why don't you pick up a few stones and turn them into bread and cheese?'

But Jesus didn't hold with such tricks. He says, 'There are more important things than food and drink. Better to die on an empty belly than live in sin with a full gut.' Well, then the old Devil takes hold of him and carries him off to Jerusalem, and sets him down on top of a great steeple. 'Now then,' he says, 'chuck yerself down from here. If your old Dad's all that fond of his only son, you won't hurt yourself. Go on, go on! Chuck yourself down!' But Jesus wouldn't have that either. He wasn't taking his orders from the old Devil.

So the old Devil carries him off to a great high mountain where you could see for miles around, farms, houses, factories, the whole lot.

'There,' says the old Devil, 'have a look round. All this land and all this property you see is mine. And you can have the whole damn lot of it if you'll come and work for me. I'll make it over to you right away. All signed and sealed.'

But Jesus says, 'You sling your hook. I've had about enough of you. I've got one master, and that master's my old Dad up there in Heaven. Go on,' he says, 'get out of it! Buzz off!' So the old Devil goes off with a flea in his ear. And a good job too.

A FEW LIKELY LADS

Now we come to the part where Jesus started doing the job his old Dad had sent him to do. John Baptist had done a good bit to clear the ground, getting the weeds out and burning the old thistles and giving it a fork over; but now it was Jesus's turn. He'd got to get it planted.

Well it stands to reason he'd need a hand doing a job like that. It was going to take a devil of a lot of hard graft. Long hours and no pay. It wasn't everyone's cup of tea. He'd set out to save the whole world from misery and wickedness, stop people mucking up their lives, and clear up the mess they'd already made.

So, first of all, he had to pick a few likely lads to help him with all the preaching and working miracles and such-like. The first two he picked were a couple of John Baptist's lads.

The first one he signed on was a chap called Andrew, and this Andrew had a brother named Simon, fishermen they were, just rough old fishermen. Andy tells Simon Jesus has taken him on, and he says, 'He likes the look of you as well.' So Simon says, 'Well let's go and see if he'll take me.' So off they go.

Well, Jesus gives Simon a good look over. He seems a solid sort of chap, so he signs him on. He says, 'Simon they may call you, but I'm going to call you Peter.'

Which was about the same as calling him 'Rocky' for that's what Peter meant in those days—a lump of rock.

Next day he signed on another two. First a fellow called Philip. Jesus takes one look at him and makes up his mind there and then. He wasn't one to mince matters you know. No beating about the bush. He just says, 'Follow me, lads.' And Philip ups and follows him.

Later, this Philip sees a mate of his, a chap called Nathaniel. He was working on a building site. So old Philip shouts across to him. 'Hey, Nat, we've found the fellow the old prophets wrote about. Jesus his name is, he comes from Nazareth.'

'Nazareth?' says Nat. 'Nazareth? I never knew any good ever come out of Nazareth, not yet anyhow.'

'Come and meet him,' says Phil. 'Judge for yerself.' So old Nat comes down off the ladder and they go over to Jesus.

As soon as Jesus sees him he says, 'I can see you're one of the best. Before old Phil called you over, before I ever set eyes on you, I had you in mind. You were standing under an old fig-tree a while back, weren't you?'

Of course old Nat was taken aback when he heard that. Because he had been standing under an old fig-tree, but there was no way Jesus could have found out. And of course it made a big impression on him, Jesus knowing that. So he ups and says, 'Guvnor, I reckon you must be the one the old prophets wrote about. You must be the new King of the Jews!'

Jesus laughed. He says, 'You're only saying that because I knew about you being under that old fig-tree!

But you wait. I'll be showing you more wonderful
things than that. You wait and see!' And he signed old
Nat on.

Soon after that Jesus did his first miracle. It came
about in this way. Old Mary, his mother, and Jesus
were invited to a wedding. And at the reception Mary
suddenly realised there wasn't enough wine to go round.
So she told Jesus, but he said it was no business of his.
But his old Mother knew him better than that. She had
a word with the potman, told him to do whatever her
son asks him to, and he might be able to help them out.
And, of course that's just what Jesus did. He saw some
old dry water-butts outside and he says to the potman,
'Fill 'em up with water.' So the old potman does as he's
told. He puts these old dry water-butts under the tap
and fills them up. And what do you think? All that
water was turned into wine. Good wine, too, none of
your old cheap rot-gut tasting more like vinegar. It was
the finest wine they'd ever tasted in their lives.

So there was plenty to go round after all. Well, most
of them had three or four glasses. And they drank a
health to the bride and bridegroom, and a health to the
best man, and a health to the bridesmaids and a health
to the old parson (and may his shadow never grow less!)
and a health to themselves.

And last but not least a health to Jesus for getting
them out of a hole. And the party went off with a right
good swing. Of course they were a bit mystified as to
how he'd done it. Some thought he had some bottles
hid under his coat, and others thought the barrels must
have had double bottoms. But most of them took it as a
matter of course. You know what people are like.

MONEY-GRABBERS

Now I'm going to tell you about the first time Jesus lost his temper. It was the time of year when all the Jews went up to Jerusalem to do their Easter duty at the Temple, and of course he went as well.

But when he got there he found the whole Temple full of money-changers and horse-dealers and such-like, cows and sheep and pigeons and God knows what, all over the shop. More like an old cattle market it was. Well, when he saw that, old Jesus got his rag out, he went pretty nearly mad. He was so wild he went off and made himself a whip. And then he comes rorting back and he chases these old money-changers and dealers out into the street, laying about him with this whip, up-ending their stalls and spilling their cash-boxes and scattering their money all over the floor. 'How dare you!' he hollers. 'Anybody would think my Father's House was a bloody super-market! Get out of here and stay out, you dirty rotten money-grabbers!' You should have heard him! It would have done your heart good!

And most of the poor folk saw he was in the right, and did the right thing, chasing all those old cheap-jacks out of the Temple. After all, there's a time and a place for everything. But the old priests and elders didn't like it. Because they were making a little bit on the side. They were getting their ten per cent for letting these chaps put their stalls there. Yes, and some of them fifteen and twenty per cent!

And they didn't think much of the way he went round preaching and holding prayer-meetings up and down the countryside either. And when they caught old John Baptist and put him inside, Jesus saw it was time to move on. So him and a few of his lads cleared out of those parts and went to the seaside around Galilee, where he'd helped them out with the wine at the wedding. And here he did some more miracles.

He cured the son of one of the most important men in the district. This old chap came to him and begged him to come and cure the lad of a fever. He'd got a sort of meningitis. Real bad he was. Well, Jesus takes one look at the old father and says, 'Go on home. Your lad'll be all right.' So the old man goes off and sure enough his son was cured. He started to get better the very moment Jesus said the words. He spoke to the father at seven o'clock and it was seven o'clock exactly when the boy started to throw off his fever.

He goes round all the villages and he preaches in all the chapels and churches, and holds open-air meetings, telling people to mend their ways and help one another, and put their trust in God. 'You've got to be born all over again,' he says. Wonderful good preacher was Jesus, you know. Not too long, and not too hard to understand, and he always hit the nail bang on the head. And folk flocked from far and wide to hear him.

He was walking by the seashore one day when a crowd came up to hear him preach. So he steps aboard a fishing boat and he asks the skipper, who happened to be Simon Peter (you remember, he was Andy's brother, they were the first two Jesus signed on). He asked him to cast off so that he could talk to the people from the stern of the boat instead of being jostled about on the shore.

And when he'd done speaking, he says to Peter, 'Let's go for a little run out to sea and do a bit of fishing.' But old Peter shakes his head. He says, 'We've been fishing all night, Guvnor, we've been at it for hours and we haven't caught a single tiddler. But we'll have another go if you say so.'

So off they went. And when they were a little way out they let down the net, and what do you think? When they came to pull it in it was so full of fish it burst wide open. They had to get one of the other boats to help them get the fish aboard, and in the end both boats were so full they could hardly keep afloat.

Old Peter hadn't seen anything like it in all his born days. He says to Jesus, ' 'Ere, Guvnor, I'm a bad lot. I'm no good to you. I'm not worth wasting your miracles on.' But Jesus laughed. He says, 'Don't you worry about that. The time'll come when you won't want to go catching fish, you'll be too busy catching men.'

And he never spoke a truer word. Because Peter didn't do any fishing after that, nor did Andy. They followed Jesus, preaching and baptising and helping him with his work. And soon after that he took on another pair of fishermen, Jim and John. They were mending their nets when Jesus called them over to join him, and they downed tools and followed him, just like Peter and Andy.

Now, when he was preaching in a nearby chapel, one of the congregation starts screaming out like a madman, as if he was having a fight with somebody. 'Who do you think you are? You mind your own business and let me alone,' he hollers. Foaming at the mouth he was.

Jesus takes one look at him and he sees the old Devil has got into him, and he orders him to come out. He doesn't mince matters either. He says, 'You come out of that poor man. Come on! Out you come! Come on, you old So and So! Come out of him! Come on out!' And the old Devil came flying out. He didn't want to, but he daren't do otherwise. He came flying out and left the poor chap alone. And more and more people came to follow Jesus when they saw him making the Devil himself do as he was told.

SERMON ON THE MOUNTAINSIDE

Now, when they saw him going about preaching and working miracles, and folk flocking to hear him, the old priests and pharisees couldn't stomach it. If they allowed him to go on like that they'd soon find themselves out of a job, especially if he went on working miracles on the Sabbath, which was their day of rest when you were supposed to sit at home and do nothing all day.

But Jesus didn't care. He just went on the same as before, straightening out cripples, curing polio, cancer, leprosy, the lot. And chasing the old Devil out of people, whether it was Friday, Saturday, Sunday or any other day. 'The better the day, the better the deed,' he'd say. And he said to the people who were kicking up all the fuss, 'Now listen, I want to ask you a straight question and I want a straight answer. If one of your sheep fell down a hole on a Sunday, would you leave it there till the Monday, or pull it out right away? Come on, answer me! And if it's right to save an old sheep, how can it be wrong to save a human being?' And they couldn't answer him. They just stood there looking at him. 'Have you suddenly lost your tongues?' he said. And they couldn't answer him. Because they knew he was right.

And one day, as he was going his rounds preaching

and laying his hands on people—a wonderful pair of hands he had, you know. Well, of course, he'd been a carpenter—he came to a mountain, and he spent the night up there all by himself, saying his prayers. On his knees all night long he was, talking quietly to his Dad, asking his advice and getting fresh power. And then, in the morning, as he came down, he saw a crowd had gathered to hear him speak.

So he stood up there on the mountainside, and he started to preach what we call the Sermon on the Mountain. And that's the most wonderful sermon you've ever heard, and no-one's ever managed to preach a better. I'm going to do my best to give you the bones of it, but more I can't do, because that's full of wonderful deep sayings, and big scholars, bishops, professors, the top men in the job, they've never done explaining it.

He starts off by telling them it's a damn sight better to be poor and humble than rich and haughty; better to be hard up and happy than rich and miserable, any day of the week. Then he says that people who act mean and spiteful, always on the make, money-grubbers and misers, they're no good to themselves nor to anybody else. The ones who don't ask too much, they'll get a proper share, because whatever they get will be enough; but those who always want more and more, the ones who're never satisfied and always on the make, they'll never know happiness, either in this life or the next.

He goes on to say that the whole world has gone rotten, rotten as bad meat, but that those who follow his teachings are like the salt that stops meat from going off, what he calls the salt of the earth. But they'd better not get too cocky about it: there's no goodness in thinking how good you are, but only in doing good to other people.

Do good to others, he says, help them and be kind to them and your goodness'll shine out like a torch on a dark night, guiding the way, showing up the holes in the road and the puddles, and marking out the proper path for those that come after.

Then he says he hasn't come to do away with the old ways and customs; he hasn't come to make a mockery of all that old Moses and Co. stood for. Well, how could he, when he's the one old Abraham and Isaac and Isaiah were speaking about? He's the one they'd promised would come and put things right.

And the way to put things right was to do what Moses and the others had told us to do: not to go killing people, not to go chasing after married women (that's not too easy sometimes, still, we have to try), not to curse and swear, not to go hankering after things that belong to other people, and not to spread lies and gossip all over the place.

But not doing things isn't nearly enough. You mustn't even think of doing them, because if you think of doing them you've already done them in your heart of hearts! And when people tell lies about you, and spread nasty spiteful gossip, don't you go around doing the same thing about them. Two wrongs don't make a right, you know.

And there's no virtue in lending someone a bob or two when you know they can pay you back. There's no goodness in that. But if you slip a chap a fiver when you know he'll never be able to pay you back, that's goodness. Put yourself in their place, he says. Do just the same to other people as you'd like them to do to you.

Now, although this sermon on the mountainside may not be news to you, it was news to those who first heard it. They'd never heard anything like it. He was speaking two thousand years ago, yet even today there are plenty of people havn't took much notice of those wonderful words and quite a few who've never heard tell of them.

He said we ought never to hate anyone, not even people who are against us. Then he went on to say if you want to do a good turn, don't go hollering about it, letting everybody know how good you are. That takes all the gilt off the gingerbread. If you want a lot of thanks and making a fuss of, that's just blowing yourself up and showing off. That'll never do.

Then he starts talking to them about saying their prayers. He says don't go making a big palaver about it so that everybody'll know what you're doing and say, 'Oh, look, what a wonderful holy man, look at him saying his prayers!' But do it on the sly, quietly. God'll hear you no matter how quiet you speak, and he's the one that counts. You need only whisper, in fact you needn't open your mouth, he'll hear you. Then he gives them a little prayer they can say every day, a sort of family prayer. What we call the Our Father. There's no point in me saying it now, because you all know it backwards. Well, if you don't, you ought to! But it'll not be amiss if I give you what I think is the true meaning of it in my own words. So here goes!

We're all God's children, the whole lot of us, and we ought to love him and look up to him, because he's our Dad. If we were all to do that, the world would soon be a better place, more like Heaven. So ask God to give you enough grub to keep you going and ask him to forgive you when you make mistakes and do something wrong, the same as you forgive people who do wrong to you; and to help you to go straight and to keep straight. Well, it stands to reason if we're not ready to forget and forgive we can't expect God to do the same to us, can we?

He goes on to say it isn't worth while bothering with fancy clothes and such, and it's no good guzzling and gormandising like an old pig. God'll look after us, and he'll look after everything alive, the same as a good father looks after his family, and the same as a good farmer looks after his beasts.

Then he has a word to say about people who are always laying down the law, who think they're always in the right, telling folk what to do and blaming them for not doing it. He says there's not a single one of us hasn't done wrong some time, no-one can set himself up as perfect, so no-one's got the right to find fault. Let those who find fault have a look in their own copybooks, he says. One blind man can't lead another blind man, he says. If he does, they'll both come a cropper.

Then he says it's no use worrying yourself too much over things. God'll always help those who need help, and give to those who ask, the same as any other father would if his son or daughter want something really badly. He says if one of your kids asks you for a slice of bread and jam you don't go and give him half a brick, do you?

And he says it isn't what you talk about that counts, but how you carry on. Those who have most to say

about what they've done or haven't done, and how good
they are, and what a wonderful pious life they've led,
going to church regular, and giving hand-outs to old-age
pensioners, and putting a couple of quid in the collection box every Sunday, they're no good, they're only
windbags. Those who do the best they can and don't
make a song and dance about it, they're the ones to give
credit to, they're the pick of the basket when you come
to weigh them up.

Then he says, 'Build your lives the same as you'd
build a house. When you build a house you don't go
putting up the walls before you've laid the foundations.
If you did, the first puff of wind would blow it down.
No, you build your house on something firm and solid,
and that's how you've got to build your lives. You take
my tip,' he says. 'Build your lives on my teaching and
they'll be as solid as the rock. You'll have something
that'll last a lifetime. You do that and you can't go far
wrong!'

SHE BRUSHED MY COAT AND GAVE MY
SHOES A RUB

WHEN he'd finished preaching his Sermon on the Mountainside Jesus went into a nearby village to get a bite to eat, and no sooner had he got there than he was asked to come and treat a fellow who'd suddenly been taken very ill. An old colonel's batman. Dangerously ill, he was. So Jesus says he'll come along right away and see what he can do for the poor chap.

But before he gets there (soon after he'd started, to tell you the truth), the old colonel sends word Jesus is not to put himself out. If he'll only say the word, he knows his man'll be cured. When Jesus heard this he said, 'What do you think of that, now? This old colonel puts more trust in me than the whole lot of you!' Then he turns to the chap who'd brought the message and says, 'Go back and tell the colonel his man'll get better before he can turn round.' And sure enough, the old batman got better, just like Jesus had said. He was suddenly as right as ninepence.

Soon after that, Jesus worked another miracle. He was going along the street when he met a stretcher-party carrying a young fellow who'd just died. And behind the men carrying the body came his poor old mother, a widow-woman she was, and the lad on the stretcher was her only son. Jesus felt real sorry for the poor old girl. He says to her 'Don't you worry, Missus, I'll look after him.'

Then he says, 'Get you up, young man, get up! Come on, get up!' And the lad opened his eyes and started to move. 'That's the idea,' says Jesus. 'Come on, up you get, there's a good lad. Get up. Get up. That's the idea!' And the lad got up and walked off as if he'd never been ill.

And news of this and of his other miracles spread far and wide. Even poor old John Baptist, who was in prison, got to hear about the wonderful things Jesus was doing and sent two of his pals to ask him if he really was the Saviour, the one they'd all been waiting for.

Jesus says, 'Go back and tell old John what you've seen me do, cure the sick and the deaf and the lame, and give people back their eyesight and bring dead men back to life again. Tell him I preach to the poor and the humble, and I bring a blessing to all who believe in me.'

Then he turns to the folk standing round and tells them what a fine fellow John Baptist was, and how he was the greatest prophet of the lot, second only to himself. (And Jesus wasn't really a prophet, at least, not in the same way, because he was the one they all prophesied about.)

And after he'd done speaking, one of the head Jews, what they called pharisees, asked him out to dinner. Jesus says, 'Thank you kindly,' and in they went. But no sooner were they sat down at the table when a young woman came up to him and started brushing the mud off his coat and cleaning his shoes, and giving him a good tidy-up.

Well, when the old pharisee saw this he said to himself, 'Fancy letting her take such liberties! If he's all he's cracked up to be, he ought to know better than that. Why, she's only an old trollop off the streets. Little more than a common tart.'

But Jesus could read his mind as if his thoughts were writ in big print. He ups and sez, 'Do you mind if I say something?' 'No, no, of course not, go ahead,' says the old pharisee.

'Well, then, listen,' says Jesus. 'Suppose a man has two fellows owing him money. One owes him five bob, the other one owes him five quid. Neither of them have got the least hope of paying him back, so he cancels the debt. Which one of them would be most grateful?'

'Why,' says the pharisee, 'the one that owed him the most, of course.'

'You're dead right,' says Jesus. And he turns to the young woman and he says, 'Look at this young woman. You call her a tart, and she's certainly no better than she ought to be. But she came up to me and she knew who I was without asking. And she brushed the dirt off my coat and gave my shoes a rub over, which is more than you thought of doing. A good heart cancels out a lot of bad living.' Then he says to the girl, 'You knew I wouldn't turn you away, didn't you! You've been a bad lot, but you're a good girl at heart. Cut along now and try to turn over a new leaf!'

And ever after that, this young woman, who some people think was really Mary Maudlin, follows after Jesus and looks after him, her and a few other women, mostly ones he'd cured of some illness or other.

And wherever he went people crowded round to hear

him. Sometimes they crowded round so thick he had a
job to move, let alone sit down and put his feet up for
five minutes. His friends tried to make him relax a bit
and not drive himself so hard. They even tried to drag
him out of the crowds by force. But he wouldn't have it.
He had a job to do and he wanted to get on with it.

QUIETENING A STORM

Now some of the priests and pharisees, Government clerks and lawyer chaps who knew nothing except book-learning, tried to trip Jesus up, you know, quoting the rule book against him—article this that and the other, subsection something else—you know how they carry on. But he always had the right answer. They couldn't catch him out no matter how hard they tried. He knew the old rule book better than they did. Knew it inside out. He'd always known it. And then some of them start spreading rumours about him, you know, the old poison pen stuff. They reckon he must have a devil inside him, else he couldn't do all these wonderful things.

As soon as Jesus gets to hear of this, he calls them together. He says, 'Now then, gentlemen, if I had a devil inside me like you say I have, how is it I can chase devils out of other people as I have done time and time again? Dog doesn't eat dog, and devils don't eat devils. There wouldn't be many left if they did! It'd be a good way of getting rid of 'em!' And he laughed. 'Now you listen to me,' he says. 'Calling God the Devil and making out that goodness is wickedness, that's the wickedest sin of the lot. Surely it isn't all that hard to tell good from bad. How do you tell a good fruit tree from a bad one? By its fruit, of course. A good man's like a good apple tree, grows good juicy apples. But a bad man's like an old crab tree, the apples are hard and sour. If I was a devil I wouldn't be doing good, I'd be doing bad. Why don't you use your common sense!'

And as he was talking to them his old mother came up with one or two of the family, wanting to have a word with him, but they couldn't get near him on account of the crowd. So someone calls out, 'Hey, Jesus! Your mother and some of the family's here looking for you.' Jesus says, 'What are you talking about, family!' Then he points to all those that stood round him and he says, 'All these are my family. They're my Dad's family, every one of them, and that makes them mine.'

Later on he goes down to the seashore and holds another meeting; and because most of them are only simple people, he tells them stories to illustrate his meaning, to make clearer what he's driving at. What we call parables.

He tells them about a fellow planting his allotment, sowing broadcast, like they used to in the old days. And some of the seed fell on ground that hadn't been dug up, and some fell on ground that hadn't been weeded; but some fell on well-dug earth, that had been properly cleared and double-trenched and forked over, and that grew up into a fine crop; but the seed that fell on stones and weeds withered and died. And then he explains that the seed is like his words, and some people are too pig-headed to pay attention to them and some are too wrapped up in themselves even to listen to them. But some take heed, and they're the ones who benefit.

Then he tells them another tale, about a farmer who planted a crop of corn. He had the finest seed money could buy, and he planted it in a well-tilled field. But the next day, when he was over on the other side of the farm, a fellow who had a grudge against him came along and scattered cockle-seed all over it out of pure spite.

And, of course, when the corn sprang up it was pretty nearly choked with weeds so he had to send half a dozen men down to weed it before he could cut it. And they made a big bonfire and they burnt the weeds, but the corn they harvested, and they threshed it and they ground it into flour. And that made some wonderful good bread.

And Jesus says, 'In that story the farmer stands for my old Dad, and the field stands for the whole world. The good seed stands for the good people, and the weeds stand for bad people. And the spiteful old man who planted the weeds, he stands for the old Devil. And the harvest is like the end of life, when good men get their reward, and the bad ones are thrown away and burnt like a load of old rubbish.'

Then he says he'd like to go for a little run out to sea. He thinks a bit of fresh air would do him good after all that chin-wagging. So off they set, and Jesus settles himself down on a bundle of old nets in the stern and falls asleep.

But soon the wind got up, and the waves started tossing the boat up and down like a piece of old cork. And the water was swishing over the side and it looked as if they were going to be swamped.

So of course they woke Jesus up. ' 'Ere, Guvnor,' they shouted. 'Can't you do anything to help us? The boat's half full of water and none of us can swim! For God's sake save us or we'll all be drowned!'

Jesus sits up and rubs his eyes. He was still half asleep, you see. He says, 'There's nothing to be frightened of, lads. You needn't have woken me up for a bit of a blow like this.' Then he raises his hand and he tells the old storm to lay off. 'Quiet,' he says. 'Turn it up ... calm down ... be still!'

And the waves did just as he told them, and the wind dropped and the sea calmed down. And Jesus said, 'Now, there wasn't much to worry about, was there?' And those who were with him were struck dumb at the wonder of it. They'd never seen anything like it in all their born days.

DON'T LEAVE ANY LITTER

You remember I told you how John Baptist was put in the cooler? Well, the reason they locked him up wasn't because he'd done wrong, it was because he'd fallen foul of young King Herod who was married to his own niece, a girl named Herodias. Well, when I say girl she was a grown-up woman, about thirty-five years old. She'd been wedded to his own brother before he took her on.

And, of course, John Baptist didn't approve of such goings on. He told young Herod straight out! He said, 'It isn't right for you to be sleeping with your own brother's wife and her your own niece into the bargain. It isn't right and it isn't proper.' Oh, he didn't half lay into young Herod!

And, of course, when Herodias heard what he'd said she was furious. Hopping mad she was. And she persuaded Herod to have poor old John arrested on a trumped-up charge, and she gets him locked up, the crafty bitch. I'd have given her what for if I'd been her old man!

But she wasn't content with that. Oh dear no! When Herod's birthday comes round he gives a party to celebrate. And there's this Herodias's daughter, young Salome, dancing in front of the whole palace, the shameless young hussy, cocking her legs up and showing more than she ought to. And Herod, who'd had eight or nine pints more than was good for him, he's tickled to death with this dancing, and he says, 'That a wonderful good dance, my dear. A beautiful pair of legs you've got! They puts ideas into my head! And I'm going to give you a present for entertaining the party. Whatever you want, you've only got to name it!'

But young Salome's got no idea what to ask for. So she goes and asks her mother, Herodias. And, of course, she knows what to ask for, you can bet your life, the cunning old bitch. She says, 'Ask him for John Baptist's head, chopped off and laid on a serving dish.'

So young Salome goes back to the King and says, 'For that present you promised me I want John Baptist's head, chopped off and laid on a serving dish.'

Now, young Herod didn't like the sound of that. In spite of everything, he's taken quite a liking to John. But, of course, he can't break his word, so after a bit of humming and harring he gives the order. And poor John Baptist's head was chopped off and laid on a big serving dish like you put the joint on of a Sunday, and they give it to young Salome and she takes it along and gives it to her wicked old mother.

Well, when John Baptist's friends heard he was dead, they came along and took his body away to give it a decent burial. Then they went and told Jesus about it. Jesus was so upset, he gathered his mates together and cleared right out of that part of the country, took a boat across to a lonely bit of the seashore where they could be in peace for a while, remembering old John and talking about him and thanking God for the wonderful life he'd led.

But it wasn't so easy for Jesus to get away from the crowds, you know. People soon got to know where he'd gone and they were after him like a pack of teenagers after these young singers. So when he saw the crowds gathering he climbed up a hillside to be out of their way. But he didn't have the heart to let them down, not when he saw how much they wanted to hear him. So he let them catch up with him.

And he starts talking to them, and he holds them spellbound with his stories, losing all count of time, till one of his mates butts in and says, 'Here, Guvnor, time's getting on and none of these folk have had any dinner yet. Let's send them back to the nearest pub so they can get a bite to eat.'

But Jesus says, 'Why don't we give them something to eat out here?' They say, 'There's not enough to feed ourselves, let alone all that mob. And no money to buy any neither.'

Jesus says, 'How much grub have we got?' They say, 'Five loaves of bread and a couple of fish, that's all.' He says, 'Right, bring it here.' So they bring it and lay it out in front of him. Then he tells all the crowd to sit down, and down they all sit, hundreds and hundreds of them, all squatting there on the grass while he takes the grub in his hands and blesses it and starts dishing it out, breaking the loaves up and putting a bit of fish on each piece and passing the pieces to his mates to give round. And the more bread he broke, the more bread there seemed to be. Till everyone had had their share and no-one had gone short and they'd all had a good blow-out. Well, some of them even came up for a second helping.

And when they'd done, he says to his mates, 'Now go

and clear up all the mess, we don't want to leave a lot of litter about.' So they gather up the bits that haven't been eaten, and what do you think? There were twelve bags of it, big bags as well, more than a man could carry!

Then they counted up the crowd, and they reckoned there were five thousand men, besides women and kids, and they'd all eaten their fill from five loaves and a couple of fish.

And when the crowd got to know how they'd been fed, how Jesus had made the grub spin out, they wanted to make him king there and then, but he wouldn't stand for it. He sent his mates off by boat and told the rest to go on home. And there he stayed all by himself on the hillside, saying his prayers, while his mates went off in the boat and the crowds went home, telling each other what a fine fellow he was, and what a good dinner they'd had. Well, you know what people are where their bellies are concerned.

GUVNOR, I'M GOING UNDER

Now, when his mates were well away from the shore, there came a gale of wind and the sea got up and it was all they could do to keep the boat afloat. They were about four miles out when the storm broke, and there they were, struggling with the oars, and the waves were pounding the little boat and tossing it high up into the air, then banging it down again to such an extent they gave themselves up for lost. And, of course, they were frightened out of their lives.

But Jesus saw what a state they were in and he came walking across the water, right up to where they were, smiling to himself as he goes marching past, walking dry-footed from wave to wave, for all the world as if he was taking a little stroll in his own backyard. And, of course, when they saw a man walking on top of the water they could hardly believe their eyes. All the other miracles he'd done had been hard enough to believe, but this one, well! This beat the band. Frightened the life out of them, this one did, to see someone walking on water as if it was dry ground. They thought it was a ghost at first.

But Jesus didn't want them to be too frightened and when he heard them yelling out, he said, 'It's all right, lads. There's nothing to be frightened of. It's only me!'

Simon Peter hollers out, 'Guvnor, if that really is you, let me have a go at walking on the water as well!' Jesus shouts back, 'All right, then. Step out of the boat and start walking.'

So old Peter climbs out of the boat and sets foot on the sea, a bit gingerly at first but pretty sure in his mind Jesus won't let him down. And sure enough, he takes half a dozen steps on top of the water, just like Jesus was doing. But when the wind caught hold of him and the waves reared up all round him, he lost his nerve and started to sink. And he hollered out, 'Guvnor, help me! Help me! I'm going under.'

And Jesus stretched out his hand and collared hold of him, and lifted him up out of the sea. He says, 'There, lad, you're all right now. But you didn't trust me a lot, did you? You might have known I wouldn't let you go under. It would have been a different matter if it had been one of them old pharisees. Then I might have been tempted!' And he helps Peter back into the boat, then gets in himself.

And as soon as he got aboard, the wind dropped down and the sea was calm again. And the men in the boat who'd seen all this, they were dumbfounded. They said to Jesus, 'Now we know you're the son of God.' And Jesus laughed. He says, 'As if all the other fine things I've done weren't proof enough. You're a fine lot, you are!'

And when the sun came up they came ashore and they pulled the boat up on to the beach and had a bite to eat. And the people living near by spread the news that he was there, so wherever he went they gathered to hear him, and ask him to come and heal their sick rela-

tives and lay his hands on their kiddies and bless
them.

Whenever he went into a village or town, they'd
bring out all their sick folk and lay them out in the
market-place on old mattresses and bits of carpet or
newspaper. And as soon as Jesus appeared you'd hear a
great shout go up—'Here he comes! He's here! He's
here! He's here!' And all these sick people would turn
and twist on their old mattresses, groaning with pain
(because some of them had been like it for donkey's
years) and they'd come crawling along the road and
stretch out their poor old arms, trying to touch his
hands or his feet or even his coat-tails, to get themselves
cured. You never saw anything like it in all your lives.

Anyhow, next day the crowd of people he'd left on
the other side of the lake, the ones he'd given supper to
the day before, they came looking for him. They'd
taken ship and followed him across the water. And
they said to Jesus, 'What did you want to come over this
side for? Why couldn't you stay along of us? We're as
good as this lot are.'

Jesus looks them straight in the eye, and he says, 'I
can see what you're after. You're after getting another
free bellyful. Can't you see there's more to life than a
gutful of grub? Bread and meat keeps the body alive,
but it doesn't feed the mind and it doesn't feed the soul.
Only God can do that for you.'

Well, they saw the sense of that, because they weren't
all that ignorant. They said, 'How do we go on, then?'
Jesus says, 'Listen to what I tell you and pay attention
to it. That'll feed both your mind and your soul. It
doesn't matter what happens to your bodies. You've got

to leave them behind, in any case, one of these days. But your souls are going on for ever. That's the part you want to pay attention to. That's the part you want to feed. My words and my teachings are food and drink for that part of you. Believe in me, follow my teachings and your souls will never go hungry, in this world or the next.'

DON'T KICK THE BUCKET YET

I TOLD you what Jesus had to say about eating and drinking, how he said the soul gets hungry as well as the body, thin and half-starved, like these little foreign babies you see in pictures where they've had a famine and they're getting up a collection for them. And how the soul needs feeding up just as much as the body, in fact more so. Well, that took a bit of understanding, that did. That was quite a new idea in those days.

Some of his followers couldn't make head or tail of it. And those who could didn't much care for it. It wasn't their idea of how a king ought to talk. A proper king ought to be talking of gold and silver, and horses and warriors and making wars, and beating up his enemies. So they slipped off and left him to it. They were fed up with it. And Jesus wasn't sorry to see the back of them. Well, they couldn't have been much cop, could they, clearing off like that? He turns to the twelve who were left, you remember, the ones he'd hand-picked at the very beginning, and he says, 'Do any more of you want to sling your hooks? You're free to go, free and welcome, you know that.'

Simon Peter ups and says, 'No, Guvnor, we're well content as we are. Whatever you say goes. We'll follow you through thick and thin.'

Jesus eyes them up and down and he says, 'I picked a

round dozen of you to be my foremen and charge-
hands. I know I can trust most of you, but one of you'll
do the dirty on me before we're finished.'

He named no names, and he pointed no finger, but
we all know who he meant, right enough. He meant
Judas Iscariot, who was to put the squeak in against him
and give him up to the old pharisees.

Now, most of the Jews went to Jerusalem about this
time of year. It was rather like their Easter time. But
Jesus and his mates didn't go because they knew the old
high priests and pharisees were out to catch Jesus and
do him in. If they could get a chance, they'd be on him
like a pack of wolves. Even where he was, across in
Galilee, they tried to stir up trouble.

Some of them wanted to know why his mates didn't
wash their hands before they sat down to eat. The old
pharisees were always washing their hands. Cleanness
came before goodness with them. But the twelve head
followers of Jesus weren't all that particular. Rough
working chaps they were, for the most part, used to
eating rough. Dirty hands, indeed! As if that mattered
a tinker's cuss! Besides, it was mostly clean dirt.

Anyway, Jesus soon put the old pharisees in their
place. He said, 'It doesn't matter much what goes into
the mouth. You've got to eat a peck of dirt before you
die. You want to pay more heed to what comes out than
what goes in. Lies and scandal, and cursing and blind-
ing and all manner of rottenness comes out of the
mouth. That's what you want to watch out for. Dirty
mouths, not dirty hands!' That soon shut them up!

And one day, as they were resting by the wayside,
Jesus said to his mates, 'What do the people say about

me? Go on, don't pull any punches. I'd like to know.'

One of his mates says, 'Some of them say you're John Baptist come alive again. And some say you're one of the old-fashioned prophets come back.'

'But who do you say I am?' says Jesus. Quick as a flash, old Peter says, 'Jesus Christ, the son of God.'

Jesus was pleased to hear that. Pleased as punch. He says, 'Good for you, lad. You never spoke a truer word. Peter the Rock I called you in the first place. And a rock you are and no mistake. And it's on solid rock I want to build my church so that the old Devil himself can't shift it. And you, Rocky, my lad,' he says, putting his hand on Peter's shoulder, 'you'll be the doorkeeper, I'll let you look after the keys.'

Then he warned them not to go telling people he was God's son and King of the Jews, but to keep it to themselves, because he knew the old high priests had it in for him and they wanted to kill him. They wanted to do for him once and for all and get him out of the way. And though he knew he'd got to face the music some time or other, he wasn't ready to face it yet awhile. Or rather, his old Dad wasn't ready to ask him to. Not yet awhile.

But he told his twelve mates what was going to happen, told them fair and square. Told them he'd be going up to Jerusalem one of these days and when he got there the old high priests would catch him and settle with him once and for all. But after three days in the grave he'd rise up and be alive again.

Old Peter didn't much like the sound of that. He said, 'Don't say such things, Guvnor, it might never happen. You stay out of trouble. You don't want to kick the bucket yet awhile.'

But Jesus gives him a clip round the ear—just playful like, you know—and he says, 'Go on with you! One minute you call me God's son, next minute you want me to do a bunk, instead of taking my medicine like a good plucked 'un. You ought to be ashamed of yourself! A great, tough feller like you!' And they laughed.

AS RIGHT AS NINEPENCE

Now, after he'd done a spell of teaching and preaching and laying his wonderful hands on people—cripples and invalids and poor sick folk and people with nervous breakdowns and God knows what else, Jesus was just about all in. Because it didn't come easy, like you might think. Everyone he cured he had to go right down inside himself to get the power to do it and that used to take a devil of a lot out of him.

So he takes Peter and James and John up into the hills for a bit of a rest, out of the way of the crowds, where they can be by themselves and get back some of their strength.

Well, when they got up there, Peter and his two mates sat down to rest and before they knew where they were they were fast asleep, because they'd had a pretty rough time as well. So Jesus was left praying, all by himself. And as he was praying, all the goodness started to shine out of his face, bright as the noonday sun. Even his clothes seemed to shine. And there standing alongside him were two of the old prophets, Moses and Elijah, and all three of them chatting away as if they were old pals.

And Peter and the other two were woken up by the glare of light, and they were amazed at what they saw. In fact, Peter, who was still half asleep, wanted to put up a pile of stones to mark the spot, a sort of war memorial. But he'd hardly reached for the first stone when a bright cloud came down on top of them, and a wonderful loud voice said, 'This is my only Son, and I'm right proud of him. Listen to what he has to say and do as he tells you.' Just like when he'd been baptised.

Then the cloud lifted, and old Moses and Elijah were gone and Jesus was standing there all on his own. And Peter and the others were scared out of their wits. They fell flat on their faces and they daren't look up, till Jesus grabbed hold of them and said, 'Get up, lads, there's nothing to be frightened of!' So up they got, and they followed after him down the hillside. And as they went along, Jesus told them not to say a word about what they'd just seen, not to mention it to a living soul till after he'd been dead and come back to life again, just as he said he would.

And soon after that, when he was going to meet some of his mates, he saw a crowd gathered round them arguing the toss about something or other. And when he came up he found that his mates had been trying to cure a poor little boy who was deaf and dumb and off his rocker, poor little chap.

Jesus says, 'Now then, what's all the fuss about?' The little boy's father says, 'I brought my little boy along here for treatment. But your mates can't do nothing for him. Will you have a go, sir? He's my only son. See if you can't do something for him.'

And there this kiddie lay, out of his little wits, rolling about like a mad thing, and foaming at the mouth. Jesus says, 'How long's he been like this?' His Dad says,

'All his life, poor little chap. We can do nothing with him. Acts that crazy when the fits are on him, we're scared he'll do himself a mischief. For pity's sake, do what you can for him, sir. We're worried out of our lives.'

Jesus says, 'If your faith is strong enough, there's nothing that can't be done.'

Well, when he heard that the old father burst into tears. He says, 'I wish to God he'd get better. And if you'll take up his case I believe he will, sir.' Jesus takes the little lad by the hand and says, 'Your Dad believes you will. And you will.' And the little boy was cured of his fits there and then. And he went off home with his Dad, holding his hand, as right as ninepence.

When his mates saw this they asked Jesus why they hadn't been able to cure the boy. Jesus said, 'Because you didn't believe you could, that's why. If you set your mind on a thing, and if you're dead sure you can do it, there's nothing can stop you. If you've got faith you can do anything. That'll move mountains, faith will.'

Well, soon after that, in spite of what he'd said, Jesus did go up to Jerusalem. He went there on the quiet, so as not to stir up trouble with the old priests and pharisees.

But they soon got wind of him and they set a trap for him. They brought along a young, married woman, whose hubby had found her in bed with the lodger. That was one of the worst crimes you could do, you know. They said, 'What do you think of her, now? Does she deserve to go on living, or doesn't she?'

They asked him that, just to hear what he'd say. But Jesus didn't say 'yes' or 'no'. He said, 'If there's one of

you standing here who's never done wrong, never in his
life, let him step up in front. He's the one to decide
what to do with her.'

And, of course, that shamed them all, that did. Because they'd all got some old skeleton in their cupboard.
They slunk away, leaving the young woman alone with
him. Jesus says to her, 'Where's the fellow that was
accusing you?' She said, 'He's gone. They've all gone,
sir. They've slunk off, every one of them.'

'Well, then,' says Jesus. 'You nip off too, while the
going's good. And don't do it again. Get rid of your
lodger and stick to your hubby, like a good wife
should.'

And time and time again, the old priests and pharisees tried to trip him up, but they couldn't do it, he was
too sharp for them. Well, it stands to reason, he was in a
different class.

A BLIND MAN SEES

So they went on trying to trip him up and make a fool of him, but they never could. At one meeting they got so wild they started pelting him with brick-bats and bottles. But he got away safe and sound by the back stairs.

And as he was walking home with his mates, they passed a young fellow who'd been born blind. So one of his mates asked Jesus, 'How does this young fellow come to be blind? Has he done wrong, or have his parents done wrong?'

Jesus said, 'He's done no wrong, neither have his poor old Mum and Dad. God doesn't punish people like that. He sent this blind boy so that I could cure him.'

Then he spits on the ground and he makes a bit of wet mud and smears it on the boy's eyes, then he tells him to go and wash it off in the pond. And the young lad goes off and does as he's been told. And when he came back he could see, clear as daylight.

And when people saw him with his eyes open they couldn't believe it. 'Isn't this the young blind fellow who used to go tapping along the road with his stick?' said one. 'He certainly does favour him a bit,' says another. 'Can't be,' says a third. 'He was as blind as a bat.' But the young fellow says, 'I'm the one you're talking about, right enough.'

'Then how did you get your sight back?' they asked. He said, 'That fellow Jesus smeared my eyes with mud, and then made me go and wash it off. And when it was all off I could see.'

Then they wanted to know where Jesus was, but the young fellow couldn't tell them. So they marched him up in front of the old pharisees, and they asked him a lot of questions but all he could tell them was the same as he'd told other people and that didn't get them very far.

So the old pharisees sent for his Mum and Dad, but they didn't get much change out of them either. The only thing they knew was the boy was born blind, and was blind, but now he could see. So then they turned to the boy again. They said, 'This Jesus is a bad lot. He's a liar and he's a twister, the same as you.'

The young fellow said, 'I know nothing about that. All I know is I was blind as a bat and now I can see, clear as clear.'

'Well, then, how did it happen?' they said. 'Now come on! What did he do to cure you?' The lad says, 'He done just like I told you. What do you want to hear it all over again for?'

And, of course, that made them wild. 'Who do you think you're talking to?' they said. 'You want to show more respect.' And they clouted him round the ear. The lad says, 'Anyone would think he was a wrong 'un to hear you talk. There can't be much wrong with him, curing a chap who was born blind.'

Well, of course, they couldn't answer that so they let him go. But they swore to get even with Jesus, if only they could lay hands on him.

But the time wasn't ripe yet awhile, so Jesus and his mates cleared out of the city and held their meetings up and down the country, mostly in the open air. And sometimes he was well received, and sometimes he wasn't.

And one day as they were going from one place to the next, Jesus's mates tried to get him to tell them which one of them he thinks is the best out of all the twelve. Jesus answered, 'Him as wants to be best, he'll be the worst, because he's liable to be big-headed and too cocky by half.'

And he calls a little boy who was passing by, a little chap about seven years old, and he lifts him up, and he says, 'This little lad's better than all of you. He's got no pride and he's got no envy. Take him as your model and you can't go far wrong. If anybody harms this little child, if anybody hurts him or teaches him to do wrong, that's about the wickedest thing they can do, and that's a fact. There's no punishment too hard for a thing like that.'

And another time he came to a village where he wanted to hire the hall for a meeting. So he sent two of his mates to fix it up, but the people didn't want to hear him. And his mates were that wild, do you know what they did? They asked Jesus if he'd let them set fire to the hall to teach the villagers a lesson. They wanted to burn the whole place down! But Jesus didn't hold with that sort of thing. He said, 'I came to help folk, not to set fire to them. Take no notice of them. They don't know any better. Let's get on to the next village.'

Next day he gathered all his followers together and picked out seventy-two of the best speakers, and sent

them on ahead to hold meetings and start setting up
their first-aid stations. He said. 'Don't ask for anything,
but if something's offered to you, don't say no. Be sure
to tell them all I've taught you. Cure their sick folk if
they ask you, but don't push in where you're not welcome. And if they turn you away, wash your hands of
them and carry on to the next place where you might
have better luck.'

A KINDLY GYPSY

Now, when the seventy-two picked men came back they were as pleased as punch. Falling over themselves, they were. Because they'd done all he'd told them to do, preaching and teaching and curing people. They'd made a real go of it. And Jesus was right proud of them.

Anyway, he was telling them what a good job they'd done and giving them a pat on the back when a lawyer chap puts his spoke in, trying to trip Jesus up as usual. He says, 'It's all very well you buttering up these pals of yours, but what about me, what do I have to do to be saved?'

Jesus sees he's only trying to catch him out, so he says, 'You've read the book of Moses, my friend. What does that say?' The lawyer says, 'Obey the laws of God and be a good neighbour.'

Jesus says, 'Right. You do that, my friend, and you'll be saved.' But the old lawyer, the cunning old stoat, was determined to catch him out, so he has another go at him. He says, 'Ah, but who is my neighbour?'

Then Jesus tells a story. He says, 'A little while ago there was a fellow set out from Jerusalem to get to Jericho and on the way he ran into a gang of rough-necks, and they beat him up and took all his money off him and pinched the clothes off his back and gave him a good old bashing about, and then they cleared off leaving him lying there half dead.

'And a parson came walking by on his way to choir practice. In a bit of a hurry, you see. And he saw this poor fellow lying there but he just stayed on his own side of the road and went on his way as if he hadn't noticed anything.

'Then an old lawyer came along, and he saw the poor fellow as well, lying there moaning and groaning, but he didn't stop either. He didn't want to get mixed up in it, or else he was scared of dirtying his hands.

'But then an old gypsy came along, one of those old tinker fellows that nobody has a good word for. He saw this poor fellow lying there and he stopped to have a better look. And he pulled him out of the ditch and cleaned him up a bit and bound up his cuts and bruises and put a horse-blanket round his shoulders and lifted him up on his old cart. Then he drove him to the nearest pub and knocks up the landlord. He says, "Here's a poor fellow been beaten up by some young hooligans. Give him a drink and a bite to eat and a bed for the night. Here's a couple of quid," he says (well, that was all he had on him). "If it comes to more I'll be along this way the day after tomorrow and I'll settle up with you." Now which one of those three was a good neighbour to the poor fellow who got beaten up and robbed?'

'Well,' says this lawyer chap, 'I suppose the old gypsy who helped him. I suppose he was.'

'There's your answer then,' says Jesus. 'Every man's your neighbour, and those who help others are *good* neighbours.' That put the old lawyer in his place!

Well, not long after that Jesus went to stay with Martha and Mary. They were two sisters, good girls,

both of them, but as different as chalk and cheese.
Martha was always fussing around clearing up and
dusting and cooking and baking and making pots of tea
and all the rest of it, while the other one, Mary, she was
more of a dreamer, thought more of reading and study-
ing than doing the housework. She just sat there drinking
in all that Jesus was saying, letting Martha lay the table
and dish up the dinner. So in the end, Martha got a bit
fed up, the way Mary wouldn't lift a finger to help her.

So she ups and says to Jesus, 'Look at that sister of
mine, leaving all the work to me while she just sits there
hanging on every word you say. And you encouraging
her! Tell her to give me a hand or I'll never get
done.'

Jesus smiles at her and he shakes his head. He says,
'What I've got to say is more important than peeling
spuds and cooking meals and laying tables and washing
dishes. Let her stop and listen. It might be better for
you if you did the same.' Putting first things first, you
see. He was a rare one for that.

Now some say this Mary, Martha's sister, was the
same as Mary Maudlin. But no-one knows for certain
and after all this time there's no way of finding out.
And it doesn't make a farthing's worth of difference one
way or the other.

Jesus didn't stay long with Martha and Mary. He was
soon off on his rounds again, preaching and teaching
and healing people and bringing fresh hope into their
lives. It was wonderful, the work he could cram into a
single day. It was as if he knew his time was short and
he'd better make the most of it.

TRYING HIS LUCK IN THE BIG TOWN

ONE day Jesus was talking to a crowd of rough and tumble in the market square, listening to him they were, and paying attention in spite of being such a rough lot. And there were one or two of the old pharisees on the edge of the crowd, waiting to see how they could catch him out and make a fool of him. One of them says to another, 'Look at him talking to all those drunken layabouts. Fancy mixing with people like that!'

But Jesus heard every word they said, and he called them over and he said, 'Suppose you had a flock of sheep to look after and when you came to count them you found one missing. Wouldn't you leave the rest of the flock while you went off to look after the one that was lost? And if you found it, wouldn't you be as pleased as a dog with two tails? Well, it's the same with me. If I can make one drunken scallywag change his way of living, it gives me the same sort of kick as the shepherd who found his lost sheep. And suppose you had fifty quid in your pocket, and when you came to count it you found you were a fiver short. What would you do? Why, you'd look here there and everywhere for it, most likely turn the house upside down. And then, if you found it, tucked into another pocket most likely, how would you feel? I bet you'd think more of that fiver than of all the other forty-five put together, just because it was lost and now you'd found it again.

'Well, it's just the same with my old Dad. He's happier over one wicked old sinner who mends his ways than over all the ones who've never done wrong. I'll tell you a little tale to show you what I mean.

'There was an old farmer had two sons, one a real steady sort of chap, a good worker, never answered back, up first thing in the morning, never did a wrong turn in his life; the other one a real young harum-scarum, always wanting to be gallivanting about with his pals.

'And one day this young scamp ups and says to his dad, "Dad, I want to go off to the big town to try my luck. Give us the bit of cash that'll come to me anyway when you're dead and gone; give it me now so's I can enjoy it while I'm still young."

'Of course, the old man didn't like the idea much, but he saw the lad was dead set on it, so he ups and gives him a lump sum, about as much as he'd have got if he'd waited for his old man to die. Mind you, it went against the grain doing it, but he did it. He said, "If you have it now you won't get it later on." And he gave it to him.

'And this lad was off like a shot out of a gun, up to the big town, and he had a rip-roaring time of it, spending money with both hands. Flashy suits, treating his mates doubles all round, going with the girls and living it up like a lord. He had a rare old time, I can tell you. But it didn't last. Before long he was down on his uppers, and he hadn't a penny to scratch his backside with. And suddenly all the pals he'd been treating were nowhere to be found. They'd gone and left him to it.

'He tried to get a job but nobody seemed to want him and soon he hadn't got a crust to eat, and he was so hungry he'd have shared a bucket of swill with a pig, if he'd had the chance.

'So at the finish he pockets his pride and he goes back to his old Dad with his tail between his legs. "Dad," he says, "I know I done wrong. I should have stayed at home along with you. But I didn't. And now I haven't got a bean. Give us a job on the farm, any old job, just so as I can earn me keep."

'But his old Dad says, "No fear. I'm having none of that. You went off with all that money, you went off and acted like a damn fool. But you came back and I'm glad to see you. Now sit yourself down at the table and get your belly filled. Your mum's baked a giblet pie, your favourite dinner. Get a plateful of that down you." And the lad sat down and started tucking in.

'Well, his older brother wasn't too pleased when he saw what a fuss they were making of him. There he'd been working his guts out while his young brother was gadding about, lashing out with parties and girls and all the rest of it, and now his old father was making more fuss of him than if he's come home in a Rolls-Royce stuffed with five-pound notes, instead of holes in his pockets and looking as if he hadn't had a square meal since I don't know when. It didn't seem right to him.

' "Dad," he said, "if this isn't the bloody limit! Here I've been working my guts out all these years for nothing but my bare wages, and here's this young brother of mine, who got more than his fair share in the first place and went and blued the lot, and what do you do? You go and treat him as if he did right to go off like that."

' "He didn't do right to go off," said his old Dad. "But

he did right to come back. It isn't what you did in the past that counts, it's what you do here and now. He did wrong in the past, and now he's sorry for it. Come on, lad, drink his health and help him to a bite of pudding. You've been with me the whole time and when I die you'll come into all I've got. But he's your brother. We thought we'd lost him, but he's turned up again." '

WAKEY WAKEY, LAZARUS, BOY!

You remember I told you about Martha and Mary, who had a set-to over who should serve the dinner? Well they had a brother named Lazarus. Now, this brother was taken ill of a fever, and he didn't seem to get any better. No matter what they tried, and no matter what the doctor gave him, pills, potions, poultices, stuff to rub on, nothing seemed to do him a bit of good. So Martha says to herself, 'There's only one cure for him. We'll send for Jesus. He'll know what to do. If he can't cure him, nobody can.' So that's what she did. She sent word to Jesus.

Well, Jesus was a long way away when he got the message, but he seemed in no hurry to go. His mates didn't want him to go, either. They knew the priests were after him and he'd be asking for trouble if he went down there. It wasn't more than a mile or two from Jerusalem, you see.

But a couple of days later he says to his mates. 'It's about time we went down to see Martha and Mary. We'll go right away.' 'Are you going to cure poor old Lazarus?' asks one of his mates. Jesus says, 'Our old pal Lazarus has fallen asleep. I've got to go and wake him up.' And of course they didn't know what he was talking about. He meant that Lazarus was dead.

And so he was, dead and buried. He'd been in his grave

four days by the time Jesus got there. Martha, who came to meet Jesus, comes running up to him and says, 'Oh dear, if you'd only got here a few days earlier you might have saved him! I know you could have done it if you'd tried!'

Jesus says, 'Don't worry, my darling. Your brother will live again.' But poor old Martha shakes her head. She says, 'Ah, but we shan't see him again this side of the grave.'

Jesus says, 'I can give life to the dead. All who believe in me can be saved. Do you believe in me?'

Martha says, 'Yes, I do believe in you. I believe you're God's son, Jesus Christ.' Then she went and fetched her sister Mary.

Well, when Mary came up she was crying her eyes out, tears running down her face. She says to Jesus, 'Oh, my dear, why didn't you get here a bit sooner? You could have saved him, I know you could!'

When Jesus saw how heartbroken she was, it was more than he could stand, and he started crying as well. There he stood, him who had the power to raise the dead and make the blind see again, crying his eyes out because he'd lost a friend.

Anyhow they take him to where old Lazarus was buried, in an old vault with a great old stone door, and Jesus tells them to open it up. But Martha says, 'He's been dead best part of a week. He'll be stinking by now.'

But Jesus makes them open it. Stink or no stink, it's all the same to him. So they open it up and there they stand. Well, first of all, Jesus had a good hard pray, because it didn't come easy, you know, this kind of work. He prayed to his old Dad to lend him a hand. Then he suddenly hollers out, 'Lazarus! Come out of there! Come out! Come on, out you come! Come on! Come on! Come out! Come on! Come on!'

And out came old Lazarus, wrapped up in his burying clothes, as lively as a cricket, as if he'd just got up from his afternoon's nap, instead of being laid dead for four or five days.

And of course the folks who saw it couldn't help but believe in Jesus after that, but the ones who had a spite against him, they went rushing off to tell the old priests and pharisees what they'd seen.

And when the priests and pharisees heard what Jesus had done they put their heads together to see how they could stop him getting more followers. They were afraid he'd get so popular that the churches and chapels would all be empty. And in the end, the only way they could think of to stop him carrying on with his miracles and his preaching and teaching was to do him in. Polish him off once and for all. So that's what they set themselves to do, catch him out on some trumped-up charge and get him strung up for it.

But Jesus's friends got wind of what they were up to and he went into hiding in a country village well out of the way. So now he was a hunted man. They searched high and low for him, they scoured the country far and wide. But none of his pals would give him away, so, for the time being, he was safe.

But the old priests and pharisees gave orders that if anyone knew where he was they were to tell them at once or else lay information before the police, so that they could knock him off and have done with it.

GOOD OLD JESUS

In the end Jesus knew it was time he went to Jerusalem to face the music. He'd kept out of trouble so far, but he knew he'd have to take what was coming to him sooner or later, so off he set, as bold as brass, though he knew full well he was going to his death.

He sent a couple of his mates to get him a donkey to carry him the last few miles, and as he rode into the city, folks came swarming round him to bid him welcome, waving flags and shouting themselves sick and silly. 'Hurrah for the King of the Jews!' they hollered. 'Good old Jesus!' and 'He's a jolly good fellow!' and all the rest of it. They were going pretty nearly mad, cheering their heads off as he rode up to the Temple.

And when he was there he got down off his donkey and started working miracles right and left. All the old, blind beggars and all the lame and sick crowding up to him for treatment, he cured them all. Hundreds and hundreds of them.

And the old priests and pharisees were hopping mad, but they daren't go for him while all the crowd was about, for fear the crowd might start on them. So they bided their time, waiting till they could catch him by himself.

Many a snare they set, and many a trap, to try and catch him, but old Jesus wasn't caught as easily as all that, in spite of the open way he went about. Besides, he had some good trusted pals—the twelve fellows he'd picked out to be his right-hand men. Well, I say twelve, but really there were only eleven, worse luck.

You see, there was Judas Iscariot, the one who looked after the money side of things, acting as their sort of banker. Not that they had very much money, only the few pounds a week the poor people could afford to give them. But old Judas's fingers itched for the feel of real money. And he suddenly had an idea how he could get it.

He goes sneaking along to the priests and he says, 'What will you give me if I help you catch him?' 'Catch who?' they said. 'Who do you think?' says Judas. Well, they could hardly believe their ears, they were as pleased as punch. They said they'd give him thirty quid. It wasn't as much as old Judas was hoping for, but you could do quite a lot with thirty quid in those days and he'd have sold his mother for a lot less than that, God blast him.

Well, that was the time of year the Jews had one of their special days, a sort of Bank Holiday, when all the family sat down to a real blow-out, turkey and plum pudding and nuts and wine and raisins and all the rest of it, a real old beano. So Jesus looks round for a place where him and his lads can have a little do, the same as everybody else, and at last he hits on a tidy-sized room in a quiet pub just off the main road. He invites all his twelve lads to the celebration, and he lays in a good stock of grub and wine. Because it was pretty hungry work, all that preaching and teaching and treating the sick, especially in the open air.

Well, when they were all sat down, Jesus ups and makes a little speech. He says, 'Well, lads, here's good luck to one and all and thank you for all the hard work you've put in for the movement. You've stuck to your guns and I'm real proud of you. But I'm sorry to tell you this'll be the last time I'll be sitting down to dinner with you because I've an idea they're on to me at last. I can feel it in my bones. But it was bound to come sooner or later, so fill up your glasses, it's the last drink I'm likely to get for many a long day.'

And of course that cast quite a shadow over the proceedings for a bit, but they soon cheered up and they drank heartily and they ate their fill, and a good time was had by all. But Jesus knew one of them was going to let him down. He knew which one it was, too. There wasn't much he didn't know, him being what he was. And they hadn't been at dinner long before he came out with it. He says, 'One of you lads is going to do the dirty on me tonight. I name no names and I point no finger, but he'll know who I mean.'

And of course they turned to each other wondering who it was he had in mind. 'Who is it?' they said. 'Who could it possibly be?' Old Peter nudges John who was sat next to Jesus, and he whispers, 'Ask him who he means.' Young John, who was Jesus's best pal, ups and asks Jesus straight out. So Jesus says, 'The one I help to more gravy.' Then he picked up the gravy boat and passed it to Judas. And old Judas pretended to be surprised. He says, 'It isn't me, is it, Guvnor?'

Jesus says, 'Isn't it?' Then he adds, 'Better get on with it, lad. No point in hanging about.' And old Judas slinks out to do his dirty work.

YOU'D BETTER COME QUIETLY, MATE!

AFTER Judas left the dinner party, Jesus turns to the others who were sat round the table and he tells them to be quiet a minute. Then he takes up a loaf of bread and he calls down a blessing. Then he breaks the loaf and gives a piece to each one of them telling them to get on and eat it. Then he says, 'When you go to church, or chapel, as the case may be, share a loaf of bread between you the same as you're doing now, to remind you of this dinner, the last we'll ever eat together.' Then he takes a bottle of wine and blesses that as well, and he hands it round and tells them to take a drink along with the bits of bread he'd just given to them, once again in memory of him.

And that was the first communion service, and ever since then folks have taken a bite and a sup at church or chapel in memory of Jesus. And he said they were to think of the bread he'd given them as if it was his body and the wine as if it was his blood, so that in eating and drinking it they were to get the idea they were eating and drinking God's flesh and blood, and then the goodness of God would be inside them. Then he tells them he'll soon be leaving them, going where they won't be able to follow him.

Peter says, 'Why, Guvnor, where are you going to?' Jesus says, 'I'm going where you can't come with me.

Not yet awhile. But I'll be sending for you later on.' But old Peter wasn't satisfied with that. Obstreperous old cuss he must have been. He says, 'Why can't I follow you now? I'd like to see anybody try to stop me!'

Jesus looks at him real old-fashioned, and he shakes his head. He says, 'Listen, Peter. Listen here, my old pal. You talk big, and we all know you're not chicken-hearted, but before the cock crows three times you'll rat on me.'

And, of course, that shook old Peter. That gave him something to think about. Then, after a bit, Jesus says it's time to break the party up, and they all go out to a lonely place where they'd hid many times before, a bit of a shrubbery alongside an old recreation ground.

Now Jesus's mates couldn't make head or tail of what he'd been saying at dinner, and they'd had a pretty hard day of it, and what with all they'd ate and drunk, they were dog-tired. So no sooner had they got into this old shrubbery than most of them flopped down on the ground and they were out like a light before you could say Jack Robinson. But Peter and James and John went along with Jesus to take a little walk before bedtime.

Jesus was quiet for a bit. Then he says, 'The thought of leaving you lads after being together all this time pretty near breaks my heart. And I'd give anything in the world to get out of what I've got to go through. You three sit down on this bank. I'll go on a little way. I want to be by myself a bit.' So down they sit, and Jesus goes off on his own.

He prays he needn't have to die, but he knows he hasn't got much chance, because that's part of the job he's been sent to do, the job he's taken on—part of

God's idea that I told you about at the very start, for
helping us out of our troubles and putting us on the
right path. God's brainwave. But he suffers agony
thinking of what's going to happen to him next day.
He's no coward but he sweats blood at the thought of
it.

Now, I told you how old Judas had fixed up to lead
the priests and pharisees straight to him as soon as they
can catch him off his guard. He says, 'I'll lead you
straight up to him and then I'll kiss him so's there'll be
no mistake. So's you'll know which one he is.'

So that same night, Judas comes sneaking into the old
shrubbery where Jesus and his mates were hidden. Of
course he knew exactly where it was, he'd been there
with them dozens of times. And after him comes a
bunch of coppers and detectives, all ready to grab Jesus
as soon as they get the signal.

Judas comes smarming up to him and suddenly kisses
him, so that all the coppers can see. He says, 'Hello,
Guvnor!' smiling all over his face. Jesus says, 'Well, if it
isn't old Judas. Come to kiss me and shake my hand in
friendship and then give me in charge!' Then he turns
to the coppers and he says, 'Who do you want?' They
said, 'Jesus of Nazareth.' He says, 'I'm your man. But
don't take any of these others. They've done nothing.
I'm the ringleader.'

So the coppers grabbed hold of him and started to
drag him away, but old Peter drew his knife and took a
swipe at one of the detectives. Cuts his ear half off. It
was hanging down and pouring with blood.

But Jesus told him to lay off. He says, 'Put that knife
up. How often do I have to tell you? That's no way to

carry on.' Then he puts out his hand and touches this fellow's ear and straight away it was joined up again. You'd never have known it was cut.

Then they marched him off, and none of his mates dared to follow, for fear of being taken. Some mates!

PETER TRIES TO BRAZEN IT OUT

So they marched poor old Jesus off like a trussed chicken, and they took him up in front of the high priest. And, of course, when the old high priest saw who it was they'd brought in he was as pleased as punch.

'Ha-ha,' he says. 'Got you at last, have we? *Now* what have you got to say for yourself?'

Jesus says, 'I've nothing to say I haven't said already, open and above-board for all the world to hear. Don't ask *me* what I've got to say. Ask any one of the thousands who've heard me. They'll tell you.'

Well, then one of the coppers who stood guarding him fetched him a smack across the mouth, and he shouts, 'Shut your gob, you cheeky sod! How dare you talk to the high priest like that!'

Jesus said, 'If I said a wrong word, I'm sorry. But I haven't. So what did you hit me for?'

Well, then they all started on him, priests and pharisees and lawyers and clerks, the whole lot, falling over themselves to nail him down. They bring witnesses to try and prove he's told lies and done his best to stir up trouble and start riots, and make a public nuisance of himself. Of course there wasn't a word of truth in it and well they knew it. And so did Jesus. So no matter what they said, he just didn't bother to answer.

At last the head high priest, the top man as it were,

he ups and says, 'You reckon you're the son of God, don't you?'

Jesus says, 'That's right enough.'

Well, when he heard that the old high priest went right up in the air. He was so wild he pretty nearly tore his wig off.

'Do you hear that?' he hollered. 'That's criminal talk, and false pretences, and blasphemy! That's worse than treason, that is.' And he turned to the rest of the Bench. 'What do you say?' he asked them.

'Ought to be put away for life,' said one.

'Ought to be hanged out of hand,' says another.

Well, then they all gather round Jesus and they start making a mock of him, thumping him, spitting in his face, venting their spite like a gang of hooligans. They blindfolded him and they bashed him in the face. Then they said, 'Who did that to you? Come on, tell us, clever-dick! There's nothing the son of God doesn't know, is there? Then tell us who gave you that one on the snout!' Then they all roared with laughter.

Now, while they were making a mock of him, Peter and another of his mates came to find out what was happening. But they kept well out of the way, not wanting to be recognised and arrested by the old priests. Well, they hadn't been there more than a couple of minutes before one of the servant girls spotted Peter. She says, 'Here! Aren't you one of this here Jesus's mates?'

But poor old Peter was afraid of being arrested, so he wouldn't admit it. He says, 'No, not me!' And he tries to hide himself in the crowd. But then another maid spots him. She stares at him for a bit then she says, 'I swear I saw you along with Jesus.' Then she yelled out, 'Here's another one of them. This here fisherman!'

But Peter shouts, 'Hold your tongue, woman! I don't know what you're talking about! I don't even know him.' And he edges his way towards the door. And on the other side of the yard, a cock crowed.

And outside, they'd built a bonfire and some of the guards and servants were stood round it, warming their backsides. And one of them comes up to Peter and he says. 'You're one of Jesus's mates! I saw you with him a couple of days ago.'

Peter looks him straight in the eye. 'Not me, you didn't,' he says. And just then the old cock crowed again. Then another fellow picked him out. He says, 'He's one of them, right enough. I'd know him anywhere. Of course he's one of Jesus's mates!'

Poor old Peter tried to brazen it out.

'Don't talk so daft, man,' he says. 'I'm no mate of Jesus. I don't even know him, I tell you.'

'Come off it,' says another fellow. 'Hark at his rough way of talking! He comes from Galilee, right enough! That's how they all talk down there. He's one of them.'

'I tell you I'm not,' says Peter, scared out of his wits and sweating like a pig.

'Oh yes you are!' says this last fellow. 'I saw you with him when we picked him up tonight!'

But Peter swears he knows nothing about it; he swears and he curses and he carries on something terrible. And just then Jesus came through the doorway, and Peter turned and saw him looking at him. And the cock crowed again, the third time.

Then Peter called to mind what Jesus had said. 'Before the cock crows the third time you'll rat on me.' And he broke away from the crowd, and he ran home, crying his eyes out.

DIRTY MONEY

NEXT morning they brought Jesus up before the Court. And of course all the high priests were on the bench, and all the old lawyers and clerks were there too, in fact all those who'd been after him from the very start.

Well, as soon as he was brought in, the old Clerk of the Court gets up and reads the charge: 'Prisoner at the Bar, you stand charged with false pretences, making out you're the son of God, when we all know you're Mary and Joseph's lad born at Bethlehem and lived best part of your life at Nazareth. Do you plead Guilty or Not Guilty?'

Jesus says, 'Not guilty.'

Then the old Judge butts in, 'Are you the son of God? Now come on, let's have a yes or a no.'

Jesus says, 'You know I am.'

Well, when he heard that the old Judge flew right off the handle. He says, 'What's the point of going on like this? He admits it. Take him away!' Then they all stand up and Jesus is ordered to appear before the High Court, because these particular old priests hadn't the power to punish him hard enough for what they reckoned he'd done.

Meanwhile, Judas, who'd acted as copper's nark and given Jesus up to the police, as soon as he heard Jesus had got sent down, he began to feel sorry for what he'd done. And he takes the thirty quid they'd given him and tries to hand it back. 'I did wrong,' he says. 'I did a bad turn to him who never did wrong to anybody and it sticks in my gullet! Take your dirty old money back.'

But the priests said, 'That's your business, mate. That doesn't matter to us. You did your part and we've done ours, and that's the end of it.'

So old Judas flings the money down, and he goes off and hangs himself. But after he'd gone, the old priests picked the money up. Trust them!

Now as soon as Jesus was brought up in the High Court, the old Judge (he was one of the head judges, this one was, Pilate they called him, he was an old Roman) he ups and asks what's the charge, and the old priests and lawyers say that Jesus has stirred up trouble against the Government, and stopped folk paying their taxes, and makes out he's King of the Jews. So Pilate says to Jesus, 'Are you the King of the Jews, my man?'

Jesus says, 'Do you really want to know, your Honour? Or is it only these old priests have been telling tales about me?'

Now Pilate didn't think much of the old priests, because, as I told you, he wasn't a Jew, he was a Roman. So he leans over the bench and he says, 'Listen here, my man. Those who brought the charge against you seem to think you've been up to some mischief, or you wouldn't be here. Now, just what is it you've been up to?'

Jesus says, 'I've broken no law, so far as I know. If I was King of the Jews, do you think all these priests and pharisees would treat me like this? I'm King of those who call me King, that's all.'

Old Pilate says, 'Then you are King after all?'

Jesus says, 'You could say I am, your Honour. I was born to be a king. That's what I'm here for, to tell you the truth. Those who know what's right and true, they harken to what I say.'

Well, that was a bit too much for poor old Pilate. Seemed a lot of fuss about nothing to him. 'Who knows what's true and what isn't?' he says. Then he turns to the old priests and he says, 'He doesn't seem a wrong 'un to me. What's the charge against him?'

Then the old priests and lawyers did their utmost to make out he'd done this, that and the other, but none of it boiled down to very much, except that they'd got a grudge against him. And all the time they were running him down, Jesus never said a word. He didn't so much as open his mouth.

So at last old Pilate says to him, 'Haven't you got anything to say, my man? Can't you hear what they're saying against you?' But Jesus didn't answer. He didn't say a word. He didn't so much as open his mouth.

And the old priests accuse him of leading folks astray and stirring up trouble all over the place, from Galilee to Jerusalem. Now, when Pilate hears the word 'Galilee' he thinks he sees a way out. He asks if Jesus comes from Galilee and they say he does. So cunning old Pilate says, 'If he comes from round there he'd better go up in front of King Herod. That's his district. He's the proper judge for those parts.'

So they drag Jesus off and bring him up in front of Herod, the chap who'd had poor old John Baptist done in. So no wonder Jesus wouldn't answer any of his questions. After a bit, old Herod gets tired of asking him and he sends him back to Pilate.

MATE, SAVE YOURSELF!

WHEN poor old Jesus was sent back to Pilate, old Pilate calls the priests and magistrates together and he says he's a good mind to let him go free. He can't see he's broken any law, neither can Herod. But the old priests start arguing the point again, in spite of what Pilate says, and at last Pilate thinks he sees a way out.

It appears the Romans had the custom of letting one prisoner go scot-free every year. Just one a year, to please the Jews at their holiday time. So Pilate offers to let Jesus go free instead of a chap called Barabbas, who was up for murder and robbery with violence and God knows what.

But the old priests weren't having that. They'd sooner have the murderer set free, this old Barabbas. They want to see Jesus strung up, that's what they want, the dirty dogs.

Pilate tries to make them see reason. 'Why do you want poor old Jesus hanged?' he says. 'He's done no harm so far as I can see. I'll tell you what. I'll order him twenty strokes of the birch, that ought to satisfy you. Then let him go. How's that?'

But they wouldn't hear of it. 'Hang him!' they shouted. 'Hang him! Hang him! String the bleeder up! Make him swing for it!'

So Pilate lets the old murderer, Barabbas, go free and

orders Jesus twenty strokes of the birch, which his men carried out, laying into him something cruel. Then they made a mock of him, togged him out in an old red coat and crowned him with brambles, pretending he was king, bowing and scraping in front of him and spitting in his face, and hollering out, 'God save the King o' the Jews!' and sloshing him round the ear and bashing him over the head.

Then Pilate showed him to the whole court and he says, 'Now then, take a look at your King!' But they weren't satisfied with that. They yelled out, 'Order him to be hanged! Hang him! Hang him!' Pilate says, 'What do you want me to hang your King for?'

They shouted back, 'He's no king of ours!'

So at the finish Pilate washes his hands of it. He shrugs his shoulders, and he says, 'Well, I did my best for the poor fellow. I can do nothing more.' And he lets the old priests have their way. So Jesus is sentenced to be hanged and Pilate orders the centurion on duty at the time (he was a kind of sergeant in the Roman army) to carry out the sentence.

And to add insult to injury they make him carry the gallows on his shoulders all the way to where they're going to string him up. But poor old Jesus is so weak he keeps tripping up and falling down, so they have to get someone to give him a hand—a young African fellow who was standing by. And as they went along, all the poor folk Jesus had helped came following after, crying their eyes out because he was going to be hanged.

Well, when he saw all these people following him and standing at the roadside crying with pity, he says, 'Don't shed tears for me, my dears. Shed them for yourselves.

You're the ones I'm sorry for. I'm going where there's no more pain and no more misery. You're the ones who've got to stay behind and suffer.' He knew the rough time the poor old Jews were to have, you see, with everyone against them on account of them doing him in.

And as they set up the gallows he prays to God to forgive the very people who were going to kill him. He says, 'Forgive them, Dad! They've got no idea what they're doing.'

The gallows was a great wooden cross, and instead of hanging him by the neck the Romans nailed him up there to die. Above his head they stuck a notice—'This is Jesus of Nazareth, King of the Jews.' Of course the priests didn't like that a bit. That was old Pilate's idea. He had it put up, just to rile them, you see. I'll bet it did, too!

And those who were standing round helping the hangman mocked and jeered at him as he hung up there on the cross. They said, 'Son of God, let's see you do some miracles now, mate! Some God he is, he can't even save himself! Look at him! Look at him up there!'

Even one of the fellows who was being hanged alongside him starts jeering at him. He says, 'Now then, mate, save yourself! Save us too, if you can!' But the one on the other side didn't hold with such mockery. He says, 'Shut up, and let him be. We deserve what we're getting, he doesn't.' Then he turns to Jesus and says, 'Jesus, mate, when you get up there along with your Dad, put in a good word for me.' Jesus says, 'Don't you worry, son—you'll be up there alongside me.'

And, of course, hanging up there in the sun he was parched with thirst. So he asked for a drink of water, but they gave him vinegar to drink. Then he looks up and says, 'I reckon my job's about done now.' Then he shouts, 'Dad . . . Dad . . . I'm coming back home! I'm coming back home!' And his head falls back, and he's dead. He's a gonner.

DON'T BE SCARED, GIRLS

WHEN Jesus died the whole earth quaked and shook like a jelly, great rocks were split in half, trees blew over and rivers swamped their banks. The graves burst wide open and showed all the coffins lying there and all the old bones. And the crowds who'd stood around watching him hanged, they were frightened out of their lives. Even the sergeant of the Guard, the centurion I told you about, when he heard Jesus cry out, and felt the earth quaking and heard the thunder, he was so taken aback and bedazzled by it, he couldn't help but change his mind. He says, 'I do believe this Jesus really was God's son. I reckon he must have been.'

Well, some of Jesus's mates and followers had stood watching at a distance, and when they saw he was dead—there wasn't much mistake about it because one of the soldiers had stuck a spear into him to make sure —these friends of Jesus asked if they could have the body so as to give it a decent burial.

A fellow called Joseph, who was on the Town Council, but had a sly liking for Jesus, he ups and asks Pilate if he can have the body. Old Pilate says, 'Certainly. By all means.' So this Joseph gets one of his pals to give him a hand and they take Jesus down off the cross and they wrap him up in a nice clean shroud and they cart him off to where Joseph's family vault is. And that's where they laid him. And they rolled a great big stone up against the doorway.

But the priests and pharisees called to mind how Jesus had said he'd rise from the dead. They'd seen him raise other people and they weren't trusting him—give a fellow like that an inch and he'd take a yard! So they ask Pilate to set a guard over this vault to stop anyone messing about with it. Pilate says they can guard it themselves if they want to—he wants no truck with it.

So the priests set a guard on this vault, and they put a seal on the doorway so that no-one can move the stone away on the sly and make out Jesus has risen from the dead. Crafty you see.

But a couple of days later, when Mary Maudlin and one or two other women came to lay flowers on the grave, they were just puzzling their heads how to shift the stone, when what do you think? There was a clap of thunder and flash of lighning, and the great stone rolled away by itself. And there, sat on top of it, was one of God's angels, with light shining all over him. And the guards were so terror-struck they fell down all of a heap, knocked right out.

Well, seeing the guards lying there and not getting up, the women crept a bit closer. They peer inside the vault, but it's all dark and quiet. So they go in and have a look round. Then they see that the body of Jesus is gone, there's no sign of it anywhere. Then, as they stood round gawping, two more angels popped up, so shining and dazzling with light that the poor women almost jumped out of their skins.

But one of the angels says, 'Don't be scared of us, girls! We haven't come to frighten you. We know what

you're looking for—the body of Jesus who was hanged
on the cross. Well, you can see for yourselves it's not
here. This tomb is as empty as a shelled pea-pod. Jesus
has risen from the dead. Go and tell his mates he's come
to life again, like he said he would time and time again.
Tell them they'll be seeing him themselves before long.'
Then the two angels vanished just as if a light had been
blown out and the women were standing there all by
themselves.

Well, they ran out that tomb like a couple of mad
women, shaking and shivering with fright, poor dears,
and they ran all the way home. And as soon as they got
there they told what they had seen, but nobody could
understand what they were talking about. And no
wonder! They were that flustered the words came
tumbling out of their mouths all on top of one another,
all higgledy-piggledy. They hardly knew what they
were saying.

Mary Maudlin runs to tell Peter and John about it,
and Peter and John go belting off to see for themselves.
And when they got there they saw the shroud and the
winding cloth for his head, all laid out neat and tidy as
if he'd just changed his clothes. But no body. And Peter
couldn't make it out—guards gone, folded death clouts,
empty tomb—he couldn't make head or tail of it. But
John began to wonder.

And when they got back and heard what the women
were saying, they didn't know what to think. Some said
they'd even seen Jesus himself walking round the
churchyard, and they swore he'd spoken to them,
saying he'd be seeing them again shortly, in Galilee.
Peter didn't take much notice of that. He saw the

women were all overwrought and excited. He put it
down to a lot of old wives' tales. He didn't believe a
word of it. But by this time young John was pretty
sure.

BOYS, IT'S ONLY ME

THE guards that the old priests had set to look after the tomb skedaddled when the thunder struck and the stone rolled away. They nipped back and told the priests. And the priests and pharisees put their heads together and puzzled out what to do about it. And do you know what the cunning old monkeys went and did? They gave the guards a lump sum of money as a bribe, and they told them to say it was Jesus's mates who'd crept up and stolen the body out of the tomb while the guards weren't looking, or else while they were asleep. So the guards took the money and did as they were told. And people who know no better believe this yarn, even today.

Now Mary Maudlin and some of the other women who'd been along to the cemetery said they'd seen Jesus's ghost. Mary said she thought it was the old grave-digger till she heard Jesus speak to her, calling her by her name— 'He said, "Hello, Mary, keep your pecker up." ' But nobody believed a word she was saying, not at the time they didn't.

But a day or two afterwards, Peter and a chap named Cleo were taking a stroll—you know, going over all that's happened and wondering what's the meaning of it all—when a stranger joins them and asks what they're arguing about and why they're looking so down in the

mouth. So this Cleo ups and asks the stranger, 'Where
have you been these last few days? Haven't you heard
the news?' The stranger says, 'What news?' 'Why about
Jesus, who was our Guvnor. We were hoping he was
going to turn the old Romans out and be our King. But
the priests and pharisees had him knocked off on a
trumped-up charge and got him hanged. Three days
ago that was and now what do you think? Some of our
womenfolk have been to where they put his body and
it's missing. Searched high and low for it, we have. But
it's gone. Not a sign of it anywhere.'

'That's a bad job, that is,' says the stranger. 'But I
seem to remember I heard something very similar before—in one of those old Bible stories. Didn't one of the
prophets say something about it?' Then he started
going over all the old sayings and promises that Moses
and the other prophets had made. Seemed to know his
Bible back to front, did this stranger, and no wonder!
Peter and Cleo could have gone on listening to him all
day. Well, they were so taken up with him they asked
him to come and have a drink and a bite of supper with
them.

And as soon as they were sat down and had their food
and drink set before them, the stranger takes the loaf of
bread and breaks it up and asks a blessing and hands it
round with that wonderful pair of hands. And then
they saw it was Jesus himself who was sitting with
them. And no sooner did they realise who he was, than
he was gone, vanished, snuffed out like a light. One
minute he was sitting there, and the next minute the
chair was empty.

Well, Peter and Cleo sat there for a little while, too

bowled over to speak. Then Peter says, 'We might have guessed who it was by the way he spoke on the road. We might have known it was him! But I wonder why he didn't make himself known?' Says Cleo, 'He didn't want to scare us, that's about the size of it.'

And when they got back and told the others about it, how they'd met this stranger and had walked three or four miles with him, talking to him, just as I might be talking to you now, and how they had no idea it was Jesus until they were sat down at the table, and then how he'd vanished like a ghost, nobody would believe them. Everybody thought they were just spinning a yarn.

But while they were all sat there chewing the rag and arguing the toss, with the doors shut and bolted, suddenly Jesus stood there right in the middle of them, as large as life. And of course that scared them out of their wits. But Jesus calmed them down like he'd done many a time before. He says, 'It's all right, boys, it's only me! Nothing to be frightened of.' But they were that scared they daren't speak or move. All of a tremble they were, thinking they were seeing a spirit.

Jesus says, 'It's me! Your old pal Jesus! If you don't believe it take hold of me. There you are. I'm flesh and blood the same as you are. Take a look at my side where the spear went through, and the holes in my hands and feet that the nails made when they hung me up on the old cross.'

But they were still a bit doubtful. Till Jesus smiled and said, 'Aren't you going to offer me a bit of grub?' And of course that made them laugh. And they handed him a bit of fried fish and some bread and honey for afters. And he sits down and eats, just as if he'd never been dead and laid out in the tomb only three days ago.

And he finished his bit of fish and then he has his bread and honey and a mouthful of wine, and they're all fussing round him as if he's only just out of hospital after a long illness and they're all as happy as sandboys now he's up and about again and looking as right as ninepence.

ONLY A FEW SPRATS

Now, one of Jesus's mates, called Tom Didymus, wasn't with the others when Jesus called to see them and he didn't believe it was Jesus they'd seen. He doesn't hold with all this 'he said' and 'she said' and 'I said to her' and all the rest of it. 'I'll believe it when I see it, and not before,' says old Tom. Obstinate old cuss he must have been. You know the sort.

Anyhow, about a week later, when they were all together again with the doors shut and bolted, going over all that's happened, suddenly Jesus is in the room again. Just standing there, shaking his head and smiling —especially at old Tom. He says, 'Here, Tommy lad, put your finger in my side. Feel where the spear went in. And look at the nail holes in my hands! Now do you believe it's me?'

So old Tommy does as he's told. Then he ups and says, 'It's you, all right, Guvnor!' Jesus says, 'Ah, ha! Pity you didn't take your mates' word for it, isn't it? There's some things you've got to take on trust, lad. You can't expect proof for everything.' Well, that taught old Tommy a lesson, that did. And that's how we come to call people like him Doubting Thomases.

Jesus showed up again later on. This time it was on the seashore. It happened like this. Old Peter and Tom

Didymus and Nat and the sons of old Zeb and a few
others, started off on a fishing trip. But they were just
about to give it up as a bad job when they saw a fellow
standing on the shore waving to them. And this fellow
shouts out, 'Had any luck, lads? Have you caught
anything?'

Old Peter and the others heard the shout but they'd
no idea who it was. They yelled back, 'No, mate. We've
caught nothing. Only a few sprats.'

So this fellow on the shore shouts, 'Throw your net
over the starboard side and see what happens.' Peter
says to the others, 'No harm in trying, I suppose.' So
they fling their net over the starboard side like this
fellow had told them, and what do you think? It was so
full of fish they could hardly lug it in. Young John
turns to Peter and he says, 'Must have been Jesus called
out to us. This is just the kind of thing he'd do.'

Well, when Peter heard that he jumps out into the
sea and swims for the beach, leaving the rest of them to
row the boat in and beach it and drag this great netful
of fish up on to the shore.

And there on the shore sat Jesus with a nice pine-
wood fire crackling away and everything laid out ready.
And he tells them to bring their fish and cook it. And
they did as they were told, gutting it and frying it there
on the open fire. Then Jesus says, 'Now then, lads, tuck
in.' And they all sat down and had a good breakfast,
sitting there together on the seashore, just like old
times.

When they'd finished eating, Jesus says to Simon
Peter, 'Simon, old son, you reckon to be my best pal and
think more of me than all the others, don't you?' Old

Peter says, 'You know I do.'

Jesus says, 'Then look after things for me.' A few minutes afterwards he asks him the same question. 'Simon, old son, you think a lot of me, don't you?' Old Peter says, 'You know I do, Guvnor.' 'Then take charge of things for me,' says Jesus. And soon after that he says to him again, 'Simon, old son, you think the world of me, don't you?' That was a bit much for old Peter. He got a bit huffy. He never could take a joke, you know. He growls, 'You ought to know. Good Lord, haven't I shown you how much I think of you time and time again?'

'Well, then,' said Jesus. 'Keep an eye on things for me, the same as if I was here myself. And now I'm going to tell you something, lad. The time will come when you'll be caught and hanged the same as I was. There's no getting away from it. You've got to follow me all the way!'

But Peter was still feeling a little bit sore. He turns and sees young John who always liked to sit next to Jesus. (Jesus used to make a big fuss of him, you see, him being the youngest, and that made Peter a bit jealous.) He points to young John and he says, 'What about him? He's your favourite. Haven't you got any special orders for him?'

Of course Jesus saw what he was getting at, and he laughed. He says, 'What if I have? It's no concern of yours, is it? You've got enough on your plate. You look after your own affairs. I've given you your orders. All you've got to do is carry them out.'

Well, after that Jesus meets up with his old mates quite a few times, and he teaches them what to say and what to do; tells them to go on preaching and teaching and healing the sick. And he says they can always rely on him to give them a helping hand and be near to them, right to the end of time.

GONE TO JOIN HIS DAD

JESUS gave his mates a promise that as soon as he'd gone, they'd get a reward and be given special powers so that they'd be able to go preaching all over the world. But he tells them to hang on for a day or two before setting out because he wants them all together when they get this promised reward.

Now some of Jesus's mates were still hankering after a new king—you know, their idea of a king, someone who'd turn out the old Romans and set up a government of his own. They said to Jesus, 'We're going to chuck the old Romans out and run our own country again. That's the reward we're going to get, isn't it?'

Jesus said, 'It's not for me to say, nor for you to know, not yet. But this I can tell you. You're going to be rewarded for all the help you've given me, and for having been good mates; and my old Dad is going to hand it out himself, so it'll be worth having, you can bet your bottom dollar. And as I told you, you're going to have great powers given to you and be able to do wonderful things.'

Then Jesus leads them out into the countryside and he lifts up his hands and he prays, calling a blessing down on them. And as they stood there, he was suddenly lifted up into the air, high over their heads, right

up into the clouds, up and up and up, till they couldn't
see him any more, till he was gone.

And as they were gazing up, two men in shiny white
clothes were stood there—a couple of angels sent down
specially to give them a message. They said, 'What are
you chaps gawping at? He's gone to join his Dad. But
he'll come back one of these days.'

After seeing Jesus go up to Heaven, they went back
and called a meeting at old Peter's place, which he
shared with the rest of Jesus's special mates, James and
John and Andy and Phil and Tommy, and old Bart and
Matt and Jim and the other Simon, called Simon the
Lawyer, and James' young brother. His name was
Jude. Funny name, Jude, isn't it? More like a girl's
name. Still, that's what he was called, according to all
accounts. They were all living together in an old attic,
and that's where they held their committee meetings.

Well, after they'd prayed for a bit old Peter goes
round and collects all the other followers of Jesus, all
those who'd been close to him, and he tells them they've
got to pick another fellow to take old Judas's place, so's
there'll be a round dozen of them, the same as there
were before Judas ratted on them and went and hanged
himself.

So after a bit of an argument and going through all
the likely names, they picked a fellow called Matthias,
to fill the place that had suddenly fallen vacant and to
make up the twelve.

Now, one day while they were sat there they suddenly
heard a roaring like a whirlwind; rattled the windows
and shook the doors, rorting round the house as if it was
going to lift the roof off. And then there was a flicker

of light, just like forked lightning, that seemed to settle on each one of them. And although they didn't know it at the time, that was the Holy Spirit of God the Father, the reward that Jesus had told them about.

And here's the marvel for you—when they start to speak they find they can talk dozens of different lingos, just as if they'd travelled all over the world and picked up how to talk like a bunch of foreigners—Irish and German, and French and Dutch-talk, Italian, Russian and Greek and all the funny languages they talk in India and Africa. If an old Eskimo had turned up they'd have been able to gabble Eskimo talk, and if they'd wanted to pass the time of day with a Fiji Islander (you know, the people who used to eat each other), they could have done it as easy as pie. It was a right wonderful gift and no mistake.

Now it so happened, just at that time, there were a lot of foreigners in the city. They'd come there as tourists, or else for business reasons. And when they heard Peter and John and the rest of them talking all in different languages they were amazed. There wasn't a single foreigner who couldn't hear his own language being spoken, as plain as plain. Proper grammar as well! Arab talk and Gyppo and American (you know, like the GI's used to speak) the whole shoot. It was marvellous!

And of course people couldn't make it out, they said to each other, 'Whatever's the meaning of it? How the devil did a lot of rough fellows like these come to pick up all these different lingos? It isn't natural.' And others made a mock of it, saying, 'They're half cut, that's what they are. That's not real foreign talk. They've had one over the eight.'

But Simon Peter, when he heard what they were saying, ups and says, 'We're no more drunk than you are. Why, it's only nine o'clock in the morning! You just listen to what we have to say—you'll soon see whether we're drunk or not.' And he goes on to tell them all about Jesus, how he'd been dead and risen again, to give us all a helping hand against the old Devil and show us the way to live. And most of those who heard him joined up with Jesus's followers. Well, the way he talked, they couldn't help themselves.

SPARE A COPPER, MISTER

THERE they were with this gift of tongues, talking away twenty to the dozen, and no-one more than old Peter! In the really old days it had been hard work trying to get a word out of him—he was one of these strong, silent chaps! Now he could talk the hindlegs off a donkey! And when he'd done telling about Jesus and how he came to die and how he came alive again and why, there was hardly a man, woman or child who didn't want to sign on. They came crowding up as fast as they could get their names taken down.

And, of course, this soon got round to the old priests and you can bet your life they weren't too pleased. They'd just got rid of Jesus, now it was starting all over again, with more people flocking to follow him than ever before. It was bad enough in Jesus's time but now it was a damn sight worse; there were twelve of them now, all preaching their heads off and healing the sick forty to the dozen, leading people out of the old Jewish ways and starting something that looked like upsetting the whole applecart. And the old priests cudgelled their brains as to how to put a stop to it.

Especially when Peter goes and cures an old man who'd been lame all his life. That just about put the kybosh on it! He did it in the church porch too, right in front of all the people.

An old beggar man it was. Used to sit outside the church selling matches and bootlaces. Couldn't walk a step. And when Peter and John came up, he holds out his tin and says, 'Spare a few coppers, mister.' But Peter says, 'Sorry, old chap, I've got no money on me. I never use the stuff. But I'll give you something better than money. I'll give you back the use of your legs.' Then he suddenly hollers out, 'In the name of Jesus Christ, get up and walk!'

And he takes this old chap by the hand and lugs him to his feet. And lo and behold, he can walk! Not only walk, he can jump around like a two-year-old! And that's just what he does. He starts hopping about and jumping up and down and laughing and shouting and thanking God he can use his old legs again, and trying them out there and then to see if old Peter had done him properly.

And when the people saw him prancing about they were amazed, and of course they asked Peter and John how they'd done it. Peter says, 'It wasn't our doing. It was your own God, the God of Moses and Isaac and Jacob, him as sent his own son, Jesus, to teach you manners and you went and hanged him. It was him who did it, not me. Hanging a wonderful chap like that—you ought to have known better, or you wouldn't have done such a thing.' And he goes on to tell them about Jesus and some of the wonderful things he'd said, and how he'd been dead and had come to life again.

But while he was talking the old sexton came up, and some of the parochial church council and the church wardens, and they turned them out of the churchyard and marched them off to the police station for causing a rumpus on consecrated ground.

So next morning, poor old Peter and John were up in front of the bench. And you can bet your bottom dollar the beak was one of our old friends the pharisees. The Jews were ruled by these priests and pharisees. They had a finger in every pie. This old beak says to Peter, 'What right have you to start preaching in the churchyard! You're not a minister, you haven't been ordained. You're only an old fisherman. What do you mean by it?'

Then old Peter spoke up. No beating about the bush. He came right out with it. 'It's like this, your Worship. We've been brought up in front of you because we did a good turn to an old cripple. We did no harm, we only did good. And we did it in the name of Jesus Christ, the fellow you had strung up for doing the same sort of thing. But he rose again like he said he would, to be along with his old Dad. And he told us to go on healing people, the same as he used to do and he'd keep an eye on us right to the end of time and give us a helping hand whenever we were in need. It was in his name we cured that poor old beggar man, who hadn't walked a step all his life. What wrong have we done?'

Well, that took a bit of answering, that did! The old beak and the priests had their heads together, muttering and mumbling, for about ten minutes. Then the old beak suddenly says, 'Case dismissed,' because they couldn't find anything they'd done wrong, you see. So Peter and John were set free. But the old priests warned them not to cause any more trouble, and to stop talking about Jesus and trying to turn the people against the law, or they'd live to be sorry for it.

But Peter and John didn't take a blind bit of notice. They just went on preaching the word of God, spreading the good news of how Jesus had come back from the dead and why, and they carried on with the job Jesus had set them to do. And more and more folk came to follow the Christian way of life.

BLIND AS A BAT

I'VE told you how the followers of Jesus carried on his teachings, and I've told you something of what they did and what they said. But I haven't told you much about the way they lived, how they put all their money into a bag and shared it out, shared every mortal thing, so that none of them should ever go hungry and no-one should have any more than any one of the others. Not that these poor lads had very much—just the clothes they stood up in and a few old blankets and a spare pair of sandals and their pocket knives and so on. That was the way Jesus had taught them, and that was the way they carried on.

But that didn't suit the old priests and pharisees. They did their damnedest to make them shut up shop, give up teaching and give up healing. And they caught a lad named Stephen, who hadn't long joined up, and they accused him of being one of the ringleaders, and they stoned him to death. Stood around him in a ring and threw great lumps of rock at him till they smashed him all to pieces.

And there was a fellow called Saul, he egged them on to chuck the stones. In fact he looked after their coats while they did it. He was the worst of the lot was this Saul. Him and his gang started breaking into houses where Christians were living and dragging them out

and getting them sent to prison on trumped-up charges.
A regular devil he was.

Well, what with him and the priests and the police,
and one thing and another, things were getting a bit too
warm for the followers of Jesus, so most of them cleared
out and went to live right out in the country, where
they couldn't be got at. And there they went on preaching and teaching and healing the sick, the same as Jesus
had done. So in spite of everything, the word went on
spreading far and wide.

Philip went to a place called Samaria, and he got a
tidy good following there. And he did no end of cures—
a wonderful good healer he was. But there was a fellow
who'd been running a little surgery of his own there,
and he'd cured quite a lot of people—though more by
trickery and quack-doctoring than by a true gift—and
he became one of Phil's converts. Or rather he pretended he'd been converted.

Poor old Phil was rushed off his feet. He had more
patients than he could manage. So he sent for Peter and
John to come and give him a hand. And when they
arrived and started doing cures as well, this quack-
doctor offered them a lump sum of money, cash down,
if they'd tell him how it was done, if they'd let him in
on the secret. He seemed to think it was some kind of
conjuring trick that anybody could pick up. He says,
'Go on! Tell us how its done! I'll pay you for it. I'll pay
you well. And on top of that I'll give you half of what I
earn myself. I'll split with you, fifty-fifty.'

When old Peter heard that he flew right off the
handle. He says, 'You go and boil yourself! Anybody
would think we were doing some sort of confidence

trick. You ought to be ashamed of yourself! Get down on your knees and start saying your prayers and may God forgive you!' Then the poor old quack-doctor saw he'd done wrong, and he said he was sorry, and Peter quietened down.

And now I must tell you some more about Saul, who had his knife into Jesus's mates and those who followed his teaching. After he'd driven most of Jesus's followers out of Jerusalem, he began hunting down those who'd cleared out and started up in other places. He hears some of them have settled down in a place called Damascus, so off he goes there, digging them out and dragging them back to Jerusalem to be punished. Proper spiteful he was, there's no two ways about it.

Anyway, one day he starts off for Damascus and he was three parts of the way there when—what do you think? He was struck by lightning. Leastways, that's what it looked like. There was a great flash of light and his old horse reared up and threw him and he came crashing down in the middle of the road and there he laid. And then he heard a voice saying, plain as plain, 'Saul, Saul, why've you got your knife into me? I've done you no wrong.' And of course he was pretty scared, what with the lightning and then this voice. 'Who's that speaking?' he says. The voice says, 'It's me, Jesus Christ, him you're for ever venting your spite on.' That shook old Saul, that did. Up to now he'd thought this talk about Jesus was all my eye and Peggy Martin, but now he began to wonder if there might not be something in it after all. But he didn't give in yet awhile. He says, 'Well, what do you want me to do about it?' And the voice says, 'Get up and go into

Damascus. And when you've been there three days somebody'll come and tell you what to do.'

So old Saul gets up, but he can't see a thing. He's gone blind, blind as a bat. One of the fellows who'd come with him had to lead him into the town. He couldn't see a hand in front of him for three days, and he couldn't eat or drink either. He was in a right old pickle, I can tell you.

WHAT IT ALL ADDS UP TO

WHEN he got to Damascus old Saul went straight to bed and lay there for three days with neither food nor drink. But on the third day he had a surprise visitor, a chap he'd never set eyes on before, sent by Jesus himself, so they say. And this chap lays his hands on Saul's head and he says, 'Brother Saul, the Lord has sent me along to cure you.' And there and then old Saul opened his eyes and he could see. And they gave him some grub and he was as right as ninepence.

But he was a changed man. Instead of ill-treating Jesus's followers, there was nothing he wouldn't do for them. People who'd known him in the old days just couldn't believe their eyes. 'Surely this isn't old Saul who used to play merry hell with us up in Jerusalem?' they said. 'If it is, he must have changed his mind a bit!' Well, he'd not only changed his mind, he'd changed his ways as well. Even changed his name. Because ever afterwards he was known as Paul, and he got to be one of the head men of the church, and he worked all manner of wonders, the same as Peter and John and the rest of the twelve.

And talking of Peter reminds me I ought to tell you about the dream he had. It was like this. He was waiting for his dinner one day, and as he sat there gazing out of the window, his belly empty and grumbling for want of food, he saw a cloud in the sky, just like a big sheet of canvas, and this cloud was cram full of grub, pigs' trotters and ham sandwiches and jellied eels and such like, all the things the Jews weren't supposed to eat. And of course they made his old mouth water, and no wonder! But he put the idea out of his head because he knew he wasn't allowed to eat such things. Then a voice whispered in his ear, 'Go on, boy! Take your pick. Give yourself a treat!' But Peter says to this voice, 'Turn it up! I'm Jewish. I don't eat muck like that. I never have and I never shall.' The voice says, 'Don't talk daft. It's all good nourishing grub. Good as any of the stuff you Jews eat. God made it, the same as he makes Jewish grub. Go on, don't be such a big nit!' Then he was woken up by a loud knocking noise, someone at the front door. So he went to open it and a couple of fellows stood there. Will Peter kindly step round and see their guvnor? He's a Roman soldier, a captain in the army. Now, Peter didn't hold with the Romans, nor did any of the Jews for that matter. But he goes along just the same.

Anyhow, when he got to the captain's house, the captain was right glad to see him. He gave him a real good welcome. He says, 'Sit down, make yourself at home, my friend.' And then old Peter called to mind the dream he'd just had and he suddenly tumbled to the meaning of it. He says to this captain, 'In the old days, us Jews didn't mix with you foreigners, 'twasn't right we should, it was against the old Jewish laws. But Jesus Christ has altered all that, we've got to carry on different now. No man's any better than any other man, I don't care who he is or what he does for a living.

Jews, Gentiles, Hindus, heathen Chinese, even the old Romans, they're all the same in God's eyes. Black, white, red, yellow or sky blue pink. Jesus came to save us all, regardless.'

Poor old Peter got stuck in prison at the finish. Poor old Phil was caught as well, and they cut his head off. And most of the other twelve were caught and killed in the end. But there were always more to step in and take their place. As fast as one was killed, half a dozen more joined up. There was no stopping them.

Well, I'm going to finish up with a few words old Paul wrote when he was in the cooler.

He says, 'Let's have a clean break with the old Devil and really get down to doing a bit of good once in a while. Let's be real good mates to each other for a change, a bit of give-and-take on both sides. Don't let's sit down on the job, but get stuck right into it and keep the fires of the old spirit well stoked up, as the saying goes. That's the way to do God's work.'

'You want something to be happy about—well, you've got it, haven't you? You've got Jesus Christ. You've got the chance to make a fresh start. You've got the chance to be born all over again. So why don't you take it? You may say, 'It doesn't matter what people think about me. But it does, I tell you. You've got to make yourself a credit according to what you believe. It's up to you to live in peace with people. Well, that's what God's told us. If some fellow you can't stand the sight of hasn't had a square meal for the last three or four days, give him one. If he's thirsty, give him a drink. If you do that you'll make him feel ashamed of himself. And don't let the old Devil get the better of you. Say, "Go on, get out of it!" Like Jesus said to him up on the mountain. "Go on, leave me alone! Push off!" Get stuck right into him.'

That's my advice too.

Sir Bernard Miles has made a
long playing recording of a
selection from *God's Brainwave*,
and this is available on the
Decca Ace of Clubs label.

ACL 324